Consider This

Consider This

• • •

Reflections for Finding Peace

• • •

Nedra Glover Tawwab

PIATKUS

PIATKUS

First published in the United States of America in 2024 by
TarcherPerigee, an imprint of Penguin Random House LLC

First published in Great Britain in 2024 by Piatkus

1 3 5 7 9 10 8 6 4 2

A CIP catalogue record for this book
is available from the British Library.

ISBN: 978-0-34944-235-8 (Hardback)
ISBN: 978-0-34944-384-3 (Trade paperback)

Book design by Shannon Nicole Plunkett
Printed and bound in Great Britain by Clays Ltd, Elcograf S.p.A.

Papers used by Piatkus are from well-managed forests and other responsible sources.

Piatkus
An imprint of
Little, Brown Book Group
Carmelite House
50 Victoria Embankment
London EC4Y 0DZ

An Hachette UK Company
www.hachette.co.uk

www.littlebrown.co.uk

For my daughters
May the words in this book serve as an anchor

Introduction

For many of us, the past few years have been a time of great change. In my ongoing attempts to use social media to share insights for coping better in our lives, I recently spent a year posting daily Instagram stories—what I called #dailynuggets. Each one was a short piece of writing meant to uplift, support, and guide us deeper into ourselves. Each day, I would pause and consider what needed to be said or who needed to hear something that might shift their perspective. Nothing was forced. All the words flowed because most of what I wrote was what I needed to remember or practice myself. The next thing I knew, I had written enough of these daily nuggets to fill a book!

Like those daily posts, this book is a tool for reflection. Most of us tend to go wide rather than go deep. We focus more on what others should do or who's holding us back. But we can't control other people—and when we try to control external influences, it's usually an attempt to avoid dealing with our own internal conflicts. The truth is, we have more control over our internal world than our external one. And how we internally view what happens to us is powerful. Of course, reflection and internal focus require that we learn to manage our feelings and discomfort about what we discover.

Not everyone wants to keep a written journal, and this type of reflection can be done with or without one. Either way, I hope the words on these pages lead you to process your feelings with intention, think deeply, and, most of all, make small shifts in your behavior as you move through the world.

By focusing deeply on your internal perspective, you can change the way you experience life. As you read these daily nuggets, some may resonate with you in a profound way, while others might sound like they are meant for another day or time. What you read today might apply differently to you tomorrow or in a year. These pages are meant to be revisited. Savor the words by reading through the book slowly, practice it daily, or devour it quickly because you can't wait for more. You will know what you need.

When my family travels back to Detroit (my hometown), we host a gathering where we invite lots of local relatives and friends over to see us. This helps to preserve my energy.

A few years ago, at a gathering, my aunt and uncle (who are not married to each other) chatted for over an hour while I observed from across the yard. He seemed to be stuck, unable to get a word in or change the topic. When he finally got away, he came to say goodbye to me. My assumption was that he was depleted after listening to her complain for so long.

Energy is contagious; sometimes, without knowing it, our energy is zapped by engaging with others. Extroverts and introverts can suffer from energy depletion. It has more to do with your social style than with the person you're engaging with.

Focus on how you feel after your conversations with certain people:

▸ *Are you restored or depleted?*

▸ *Are you anxious or at ease?*

▸ *Did you learn something new about yourself or the other person?*

▸ *Did you feel comfortable with the topic?*

▸ *Were you triggered by something they said?*

▸ *Did you enjoy the conversation?*

▸ *What would you like to do differently if you had to talk to this person again?*

● ● ●

I remember when "No New Friends" came out. I liked it. The song was catchy, and I got what Drake was saying, but I didn't agree with it. I was joking with someone and told them I think I need to make one new friend every year just in case any of the friendships I have don't work out. But seriously, it's important to constantly build friendships.

So here are some ideas on how to do that:

- **Consider cross-generational friendships.** *When we're growing up, a great deal of the friends we make are through school, so our friends are always around our age. As adults, whether it's in the workplace or at the gym, we can explore the possibility of having friends of a variety of ages.*

- **Don't be deterred by differences in lifestyle.** *Sometimes we let things like having or not having kids stop us from starting a friendship before we've really even tried. There are so many things that you could potentially have in common with a person. Don't let a lifestyle difference act as a barrier to building a friendship.*

- **Be open to making friends in a variety of ways.** *You can meet a friend anywhere. At work, in a class, even at the grocery store. Maybe you have a friend who wants to introduce you to someone they think you'll really hit it off with. It might not work out, but it could be a match made in friendship heaven. Don't limit yourself.*

- **Bring your online connections offline.** *If you find yourself exchanging messages with someone on social media consistently, try building on that relationship. Exchange phone numbers, and see how your dynamic evolves in the real world.*

• • •

While in grad school, I noticed that finals affected me by causing my eye to twitch. It would start right around when a paper was due and wouldn't stop until a day or so after I turned it in. That's when I learned that waiting until the last minute to meet a deadline wasn't good for me. Some people work better under pressure, but I'm terrible at pulling all-nighters.

Eye twitching and headaches are ways my body lets me know I'm stressed out. From time to time, when this stress indicator returns, I evaluate what's happening in my life and determine how I need to shift.

So listen to your body.

It's communicating how you feel and what you need.

If you have a headache, wonder what caused it.

If you have a rash, see if you can find out what caused it. See a doctor.

If you become anxious in someone else's presence, wonder why.

Stomachaches, panic attacks, nausea, sweating, headaches, stuttering, and twitches are warning signs from your body. Listen and decipher the message.

Stress manifests as physical symptoms. Please don't ignore them.

●　●　●

Sometimes, just sharing can seem like bragging when the people you're sharing with aren't fulfilled in their own lives. You may not know what someone is experiencing, but when you do know, consider the audience.

Sharing your achievements with others isn't bragging unless you do it to one-up others. Your audience and the timing both matter.

CONSIDER THIS:

Is this the appropriate time to share?

Considering the person and their situation, should I tell them about my good fortune?

When it's a delicate situation, such as sharing a pregnancy with a friend who has fertility issues, you will have to deal with any potential discomfort that follows your disclosure. Even when you aren't bragging, some information might be complex for others to receive.

● ● ●

There are some people I miss, yet I'm also more at peace because I no longer have a relationship with them.

If you guilt yourself for not wanting to keep every relationship, you might hold on to some people for too long. Sometimes, you are indeed better off without some folks because you can't be the best version of yourself with them in your life. Perhaps it isn't just them; it's you in combination with them. But still, some relationships are just not a good fit, not what you need, and not meant to last.

Relationships teach you who you are. They hold so much valuable information, so use them to pay more attention to yourself.

Notice what you like and don't like.

Notice how you feel around specific people.

Notice your growth.

Notice when you need to challenge yourself to change.

Not paying attention to what you need to learn about yourself will lead you to similar relationship dynamics in the future. It will be the same thing all over again.

● ● ●

The difference between holding a grudge and holding a boundary is the following: Am I trying to teach someone a lesson, or am I keeping myself safe and comfortable in this relationship?

Boundaries are not weapons, and they are not tools to control others.

● ● ●

Years ago, I invited a friend over for a game night. She brought a friend, who seemed not to like me. The friend engaged more with others and was short with me. I remained pleasant but knew we weren't a match. A friend of my friend may not become my friend.

Get more comfortable with the fact that not everyone will like you.

Once you embody the idea "I am not for everyone," you will feel less offended when you discover that someone is not for you.

It's hard to accept this (I know), but it's also hard to get everyone to like you. Working to be liked is exhausting and ineffective. What people like about you is unique to them, and what they dislike about you is about them.

● ● ●

W atch me." This is something kids say to bid for affection and attention from their caregivers.

You likely said it as a child, and you likely still desire to be seen now.

Everyone wants to be seen.

Everyone wants to be celebrated.

Seeking compliments is a way of wanting to be seen.

Wanting to be seen and heard by others is human.

● ● ●

Critical thinking is an essential life skill.

Our mental health is diminished when we absentmindedly follow what we see without deep thought.

If you see something on social media or the internet, or you hear a suggestion that doesn't work for your situation, don't apply it.

Most advice is general, and everything mentioned won't fit your individual needs.

● ● ●

A nxiety can cloud your judgment with unrealistic, improbable worry. When you're anxious, it's easy to believe anything is possible. For example, you might think, "If I fly, the plane will crash." While this is possible, it's statistically improbable.

Distinguishing what's possible from what's probable can help reduce your anxiety.

While it's tough to do when you are experiencing anxiety, try to listen carefully to what you think and say whenever you feel ambivalent, suspicious, or confused. You may feel resistant to this, but things that are good for us can feel like a bad idea when we feel anxious.

Ask Yourself:

▸ *Is this dangerous, or am I afraid and possibly anxious?*

Anxiety makes things seem unsafe. When this happens, you have to determine the difference between anxiety-based fear that is unfounded versus fear that is founded in reality.

● ● ●

E motional neglect is when we don't get enough emotional support when we need it from those we desire it from. When this happens, one result is that we often fail to ask for what we need. And when we do, we feel like we're imposing on the other person.

If you were brought up emotionally neglected, you will likely feel guilty when you speak up for yourself and your needs. But this guilt doesn't mean you're doing anything wrong. It simply means that expressing your needs is new and uncomfortable for you.

You deserve to have people meet your needs.

You can overcome the impact of not having your needs met in the past.

You can find trustworthy sources for emotional support.

If others have made you feel guilty for having needs, it means they weren't able to meet those needs. It doesn't mean no one can meet them.

● ● ●

My life changed when I started pursuing peace.

I no longer want to be in complicated or chaotic relationships.

Give me ease, please.

Sometimes, we get used to things that aren't good for us, such as ongoing chaos. Pivot away from what may have become an unhealthy norm, and move toward peace.

• • •

S top being hard on yourself for taking too long to express your needs.

While waiting, you are gaining courage and building your tolerance for pushback.

Things are hard to say because they can't be unsaid, so they can sometimes change a relationship. Therefore, it makes sense to be careful about what you say.

When you don't feel emotionally safe enough to speak up, it's especially hard to express what you need to express.

Things are hard to say when you've spoken up in the past and weren't heard.

Things are hard to say when speaking up is tethered to consequences.

Be kind to yourself when you struggle to say hard things.

● ● ●

Nurture yourself as you would a small child.

The little version of you still needs many things you think you stopped needing.

Be gentle.

Be patient.

Be present.

Be warm.

Speak to yourself kindly, as if you are precious . . . because you *are* fragile.

You never outgrow needing tender love, but perhaps you stopped receiving it. Give it to yourself now.

You are soft, and you deserve to be nurtured.

● ● ●

B elieving that you know everything is limiting.

Information changes over time, systems get updated, or you just don't have all the details.

Be open to learning from anyone or any place.

When you aren't willing to learn, you no longer grow.
You become stagnant.

The key to growth is lifelong learning.

▸ *What's something you recently changed your opinion about?*

▸ *What new habit or belief have you tried on for size?*

• • •

When you utter the words "you should," you walk down the path of dispensing advice.

Notice how often you give advice when someone mentions a problem they are having. Try focusing less on a solution and more on listening to them. This can relieve the pressure that you have to give them the "right" answer.

CONSIDER THIS:

Practice waiting for someone to ask your opinion before offering suggestions.

People love to vent, and sometimes they just want you to listen.

Ask Yourself:

▸ *Why do you feel the need to solve their problems for them?*

▸ *Who wants to hear your opinion, and who wants you to listen?*

• • •

I've been a hard-core fan of a few people who have fallen from grace. Those people taught me:

Admire people, but don't idolize them.

People aren't perfect, and we tend to forget they're human when we idolize them. Placing people on pedestals implies that they are more capable of perfection than the rest of us. They are not.

When you enjoy or admire the work of someone, separate who they are from the perfection-driven perspective.

● ● ●

In our attempt to make sense of things, we sometimes say, "Everything happens for a reason."

Not everything happens for a reason.

Some things happen for a reason.

Some things are senseless.

It's hard to comprehend that something can occur for no reason we'll be able to understand.

When we say "Everything happens for a reason," it can dismiss our feelings or the feelings of others.

It's okay to say "I don't know why this happened, and it hurts."

Feel your feelings without immediately trying to make sense of an experience.

● ● ●

S ometimes, people learn to protect themselves by acting tough, mean, or standoffish.

Being guarded is a sign of hurt.

Learning to trust is scary, but not trusting is lonely.

While meanness is a method of protection, it keeps everyone away, even the good people. When you want closeness, you must apply soft skills and leave the tough (protective) ones behind.

● ● ●

You will not master or know everything before you start.

Opportunities will be presented before you feel 100 percent ready.

Most things in life require on-the-job training, whether relationships, parenting, or work.

Be willing to learn as you go. It's okay to make mistakes along the way. That's part of the learning process.

● ● ●

Clear is kind.

—Brené Brown

I'm not good at being direct" means "I fear how others will respond" or "I want people to figure it out without having to do anything that might make me feel uncomfortable."

When we are indirect, people aren't allowed to respond. It's unfair to assume that the response will be negative without giving equal weight to the possibility that someone will appreciate that we have been forthcoming.

You are not a mind reader, so it's usually inaccurate to assume you know how someone else will react.

Be direct as a means of clear communication. Let go of the notion that people should and will figure it out on their own.

● ● ●

Each relationship is unique. People are not the same.

If you apply a one-size-fits-all approach to your relationships, someone isn't getting what they need.

You can sometimes be more flexible with your boundaries with certain people.

In other cases, you will need to state your boundaries explicitly.

Treat people according to who they are, not how everyone "should" be.

• • •

I didn't do it."

We might say this even if it's a lie.

Lying may protect the way others view us, but it also makes us appear unreliable and untrustworthy.

Sometimes, when we do something we can't live with, we refuse to take responsibility for our actions. This is an attempt to protect our ego.

When we can't accept the bad, mean, or destructive ways we harm others, we might protect ourselves by blaming someone else or denying responsibility.

Awareness, acceptance, and accountability often push us to be more honest.

● ● ●

In this lifetime, I've been many versions of myself. All iterations were relevant at times. Clinging to who we once were can hold us back from who we're becoming.

Old Me:

▸ *Loved talk shows*

▸ *Would help people before they asked*

▸ *Listened to music full blast*

▸ *Picked pink as my favorite color*

▸ *Wanted to be a detective after watching lots of episodes of* Law and Order, *and even changed my major to criminal justice*

New Me:

▸ *Can't commit to watching any show that airs daily*

▸ *Is selective about the people I help and when*

▸ *Listens to podcasts, audiobooks, and music (in that order)*

▸ *Likes so many colors that I can't pick one favorite*

▸ *Rarely watches* Law and Order

Embrace the shifts in who you are.

Allow yourself to step away from the old you gracefully.

You don't have to be who you were last year, last week, or yesterday.

When you push against changes that are naturally occurring, you delay progress.

From time to time, ask yourself:

▸ *Who was I?*

▸ *Who am I becoming?*

● ● ●

A fter you end an unhealthy relationship, your mind will inevitably remember the moments when you felt hurt.

It might seem like forgetting would be easier, but remembering may caution you to avoid tolerating similar behavior in the future.

Memories are a gift to the present and can center you in clarity.

● ● ●

E fficiency and time management are excellent skills to learn, but when you have too much to do, they won't help. Sometimes, you need to unload your plate instead of making everything fit.

Distinguish between a necessary choice (I have to) and an optional choice (I should). Managing too many things without discernment will keep you in a cycle of feeling overloaded.

Doing less is the ultimate time-management and efficiency skill.

● ● ●

You have always needed others. You might get better at doing things alone when no one is available, but from the moment you were born, you looked to others for care.

If your needs weren't honored in the past, expressing them to someone else may now feel uncomfortable.

So if you've lost the courage to ask for what you need, REMEMBER THIS:

▸ *There are new people in your life who are different from the people in your old relationships.*

▸ *When you are healthier in your interactions, you meet people who can care for you in new ways.*

Reclaim your voice, and ask for what you need.

● ● ●

Comparing is sometimes a good thing. It can be a natural way of determining who you are and what you want.

The dark side of comparison is when you measure yourself against others and become malicious, depressed, anxious, or resentful. There will always be someone who has more than you or does more than you, and comparing yourself with them will cause chronic discontent.

On the other hand, seeing what others have can motivate you to improve, set new goals, make life changes, or find a greater appreciation for what you have.

Comparison can be the thief of peace and contentment, or it can motivate you to seek your own version of joy.

● ● ●

H armony in boundaries is saying both yes and no strategically, not always saying one or the other.

There may be certain people you frequently say yes to and others you often say no to.

You can be flexible with saying yes or no based on the person making the request, the day, your need for rest, your need to do more, and so on.

Before answering, survey your life to determine what can and can't fit into what already exists.

Notice what you'll need to shift to accommodate a request.

Pause before answering.

Boundaries can be adjusted according to your life needs.

● ● ●

While I prepared a pot of spaghetti, a friend told me exactly how spaghetti should be made. However, according to a quick search on the internet, there are various ways to prepare the dish.

There is more than one way to do most things—multiple paths to a destination.

When we argue about the supposed "right" or "wrong" way to do something, it's usually a disagreement about preference.

Practice Saying This:

"My preference is . . ." instead of "I'm right."

● ● ●

E nabling is rooted in profound caring and trying to fix, as well as a feeling of powerlessness.

Watching a loved one suffer can be unbearable, and doing something to save them from their despair feels like caring even when it's self-depleting.

It takes time to learn how to offer as much help as possible without depleting yourself.

Once you recognize that you can't possess power over others, you will move away from your role as a fixer.

Care without becoming consumed by it.

● ● ●

There is no right or wrong way to feel.

When others feel one way, we might feel differently, which doesn't mean there's anything wrong with how we feel.

We complicate feelings when we start to judge them as good or bad and weigh them against what others are feeling.

If we want to grow, we need to stop asking others to match our feelings. Sometimes, they can't, which doesn't mean we need to change ours.

We don't have to feel like everyone else for our feelings to be meaningful.

Trusting that our feelings are unique allows us to express our emotions freely.

● ● ●

You want to be considerate, but you can't always consider others.

You can want people to be happy, but you can't promise your behaviors will make them happy.

Healthy people-pleasing is what you are willing to do for a relationship without harming yourself or constantly sacrificing your own needs.

Unhealthy people-pleasing is when you rarely say no, give when you can't, and sacrifice to your detriment.

Healthy people-pleasing won't lead to resentment and can be positive for your relationships.

Please others but know when you're giving too much.

● ● ●

M istakes are a significant part of learning, and you will make plenty of them.

Remember to be kind to yourself for not getting it right while you are still learning.

Remember to be kind to yourself when you break a rule; perhaps you need to learn some more.

Humans make mistakes.

Wise humans learn from mistakes.

Gentle humans are kind to themselves and others when mistakes are made.

Growing humans say, "I will make mistakes as a part of my learning process."

• • •

J ealousy is normal, but it can be an uncomfortable emotion.

When you feel jealous, do this:

▸ **Acknowledge:** *"I feel jealous."*

▸ **Wonder why:** *"I feel jealous because . . ."*

Don't do this:

▸ *Make others believe they need to have less or be less to make you feel comfortable.*

▸ *Sabotage someone else's moment.*

▸ *Diminish what someone else has.*

▸ *Pretend that you aren't jealous.*

Thought shift: People will have things and achieve things that are different from what you have or have achieved. You, too, are unique and will have something different and succeed in ways others can't.

We are all different, and it doesn't make sense to compare.

● ● ●

L oving yourself (self-love) will always be a part of the wellness conversation.

Many of us have a hard time giving to ourselves regularly. The terms used have shifted from "self-love" to "self-care" to "self-nurturing," but they all mean to be good to yourself.

It's helpful to wonder:

▸ *Who made you believe that nurturing yourself was selfish?*

▸ *Was it someone who regularly neglected themselves?*

▸ *Was it someone trying to push you to do something for them?*

Nurturing yourself might look like this:

▸ *Resting when you're sick, or taking an extra day after a vacation to relax*

▸ *Leaving the laundry in the basket overnight*

▸ *Going to bed early or sleeping in*

What you need is not what someone else might need.

Therefore, they can only assume what might work for you.

Every moment of the day, you are with yourself. Lovingly ask yourself, "What do I need now?"

● ● ●

An easy life isn't promised.

In some capacity, discomfort is a part of life for most of us.

Although uncomfortable, feeling challenged is life-changing.

Creating your dream life or ideal relationships involves some level of risk. So do things that make you uncomfortable when there's potential within them to improve your life.

● ● ●

L earn to manage your energy, not match someone else's energy.

Matching energy can look like this:

▸ *When people are mad at you, you become angry at them.*

▸ *When someone doesn't reply to your text immediately, you return the same energy and make them wait.*

When you do as they do, you are operating on someone else's energy. This has been known as "giving people a taste of their own medicine."

Examine the situation, and be honest with yourself about your feelings: "I'm hurt," not "I'm hurt, so I will hurt them back."

When you are hurting or disappointed, feel it but don't take that pain out on someone else.

Decide to follow *your* energy, not match anyone else's.

● ● ●

Forgiveness is forward motion.

Forgiveness means you don't allow anyone to hold power over your life in the present, over who you are, or over what you become.

It doesn't mean you condone inappropriate behavior, but releasing the hold that someone or something has over you helps you move on.

The best way to forgive is to take small steps forward in your life. When you are no longer bound by what happened, it's a sign of forgiveness.

Freedom is forgiving others even if they have not apologized, simply because it sets you free.

● ● ●

L etting go is hard, but it can also be what's best. When you stay attached to something or someone beyond the point of usefulness, you rob yourself of the space for more suitable people, things, and experiences.

Allow people to leave when they say they want to go.

Perhaps you're afraid to be alone, but if the other person wants something different, holding on won't give you what you need.

Move toward where you're wanted.

● ● ●

When we aren't ready to change or make a hard choice, we often protect ourselves by saying, "Things aren't so bad."

It's hard to see what's right in front of you when you don't want something to be true.

You don't want to see what you aren't ready to handle.

When something feels off, pay attention to what you've been ignoring.

● ● ●

M astery or excellence comes with consistent practice. Yet some of us want to skip the learning process and breeze into an expert level. We might forget how hard it is to not be good at something. Then, whenever we face anything challenging, we want to quit.

Reminder:

▸ *You are not a failure; you're learning something from scratch.*

▸ *Processing new information takes time.*

▸ *With practice, you will likely improve.*

▸ *You were once terrible at many things (walking, eating with utensils, writing your name, etc.).*

TRY THIS:

Find something you aren't good at and practice until you become better.

Do something new as a practice of remaining humble.

It's healthy to not be good at everything.

● ● ●

L abel your feelings.

A therapist's favorite tool is a feelings chart. It helps us (and you) understand what you feel. Situations that are hard to manage become more manageable when you have the words to describe your feelings. Without clarity, you remain in limbo, maybe repeating something like "I don't know what I feel."

For instance, when your mind is racing about a topic, name the ruminating behavior:

▸ *I am anxious.*

▸ *I am worried.*

▸ *I'm hypervigilant.*

Putting words to what you're feeling helps remove the mystery about it.

Ask yourself what your feelings are attempting to reveal:

I don't want to _____.

I need more _____.

I want less _____.

Developing your language skills will help you communicate and respond.

● ● ●

B irthdays are my sacred personal holiday. Early on, I would wait for a friend or romantic partner to plan something for me. I was mad if they didn't. Yet, I was also mad if they did plan something that wasn't exactly what I secretly wanted. I thought they "should have known better." Either way, I was giving the power of something meaningful to me over to someone else to figure out.

Now, in order to be fair to others and myself, I plan my own celebration or clearly state my expectations to the person planning it. This practice has kept me from feeling sad on my birthday.

People will constantly disappoint you when you expect them to meet needs that you haven't made clear to them.

Sometimes, we test people to see how much they love or care about us. But is it fair to test someone when they don't fully know our needs?

Clarity saves relationships.

● ● ●

Anxiety can be a mental health diagnosis, or it can be a human emotion. Everyone feels anxious at some point. Giving words to our feelings helps us connect with others and explore our emotions.

Anxiety isn't new; it's always been there. At times, it's helpful because it serves as a warning sign. At other times, it's unhelpful because it stops us from doing something that could be good for us.

Others feel anxious, too, and connecting with them can help us feel less alone. Naming and sharing allow others to understand our behavior. When people don't know we're anxious, they can't empathize with us for canceling plans at the last minute, not wanting to talk, or being afraid to act. Let them know why.

It can be helpful for our mental health and relationships to be transparent with others about our anxiety.

● ● ●

In many movies, it's a common theme that when parents travel, kids throw secret parties. Certainly, we've all had moments when we did things that weren't supervised. As adults, we are our own supervisors or enforcers.

Therefore, choose to do the right thing when no one is watching.

When no one is watching, I still choose to

▸ *Pick up after myself*

▸ *Speak kindly to myself*

▸ *Return things that don't belong to me*

▸ *Leave kind comments on social media*

COMPLETE THIS: When no one is watching, I still choose to

_____.

Your character is present when you don't have to make the right choice but still choose to act with integrity.

● ● ●

*C*urb *Your Enthusiasm* is one of my favorite television shows. Each episode is centered on a small but "big deal" moment for Larry David. In season 10, episode 1, Larry gets into an argument with a coffee shop owner over whether his coffee is hot enough. He goes as far as putting his nose into a friend's coffee to test the temperature.

Larry often finds himself in predicaments that genuinely annoy him, while others seem to be at ease in similar situations. But that doesn't mean his experiences aren't a big deal for him.

You are a big deal, and what happens to you is a big deal.

Sometimes, people can't see your life experiences as a big deal because they are coping with their own big-deal stuff.

You matter, even when people cannot recognize what you are going through.

● ● ●

Learning from experience is a way to gain valuable information. However, when we know how something will turn out, we often try to protect people from the work of learning through experience. Telling someone "Trust me, I know," isn't as effective as it would be for them to figure it out on their own.

What are some things you had to learn for yourself?

Energy and time are lost trying to save people from issues they continuously create. It's more peaceful to allow people to sit in the lives they construct than to try to get them to live differently. Some people will make poor choices and never learn their lesson.

It's hard to watch people suffer, but sometimes you can't do anything about it.

● ● ●

Other people's opinions of you can shape what you think about yourself and who you become. No matter how many friends tell you to ignore the negative feedback, you can't unhear what was said.

Nevertheless, the most significant opinion is the one you have of yourself. When you start to believe and live as if you are what other people say, you rob yourself of the freedom to live your life on your own terms.

Ask Yourself:

▸ *How do I choose to show up in the world?*

▸ *What new beliefs do I need to incorporate about my self-image?*

• • •

L et us unlearn that self-neglect is a sign of how much we care or how important something is to us. We can love and care for others while caring for ourselves.

When I became a parent, people cautioned me to give up my hobbies. They told me that parenting involves letting go of personal desires, such as hair maintenance or time with friends.

On the contrary, parenting has shown me what matters. For instance, I'm much more pleasant when I take a few minutes in the morning before everyone else wakes up to have a cup of tea and enjoy some quiet time. Parenting has helped me prioritize my time with friends and family who feed my spirit.

Giving up who we are is not a sign of love; it's a symptom of neglect. Perhaps it isn't parenting that causes self-neglect for you. It could be a demanding job, caring for your parents, or transitioning into a new relationship. Remember to always do the things that fill you up.

Our efforts for others go further if we show up rested, nourished, and replenished.

● ● ●

In high school, I received bad advice from a friend's well-meaning mother. She told me to date someone who liked me more than I liked him. That doesn't sound so bad, right? Her advice didn't work for me, however. When I tried dating someone who liked me more, I felt terrible because I could never catch up to how he felt in the relationship.

Later, I realized my friend's mother was trying to convey "Keep the ball in your court to avoid being hurt." But I ended up hurting the other person instead, and that, in turn, hurt me. Love is not a game, and one person shouldn't hold all the leverage.

Some of the people you love dearly are well-intentioned. However, there might be better advice for you. Patiently listen, but don't apply poor advice.

● ● ●

You will watch others have fun doing things that may not suit you. Perhaps those activities aren't a good fit for you right now, or maybe they never will be.

Learn to watch people do things without having to experience the same thing. You will find that when you engage in activities that aren't aligned with you, you won't genuinely enjoy yourself. Some things are for you, and some are best watched from afar.

You are not missing out on things that aren't a good fit for your personality, interests, or lifestyle.

Think beyond the moment, and consider your own preferences, not what appears good for others.

● ● ●

There may be some truth in statements about how we behaviorally resemble others. "You act like your mother" is a broad statement, but perhaps there's a small piece of truth in it. It can be helpful to wonder or ask "How do I act like my mother?" Others can see what we don't see in ourselves. We may see ourselves as how we'd like to be.

During my wedding weekend, so many people commented on how I'm just like my mom. They meant "You and your mom love to socialize." The observation was accurate, but I didn't realize that's the way they meant it. If someone said something negative, such as "Your temper is like your father's," that might be more challenging to consider. But before dismissing the possibility, consider if it's likely they're right.

It's hard to see ourselves in others.

Notice yourself becoming upset, frustrated, or mad at people for doing things you've done yourself.

Where can you apply grace in these situations?

People show us who we are, as well as the areas in which we need to grow.

● ● ●

S trict rules you keep can become walls that disconnect you from others. If the goal is connection, reexamine the rules you follow that keep you disconnected. The structures you create for your life to be safe should only keep harmful people away, not everyone.

Self-prescribed rules are not the law, and they don't need to be followed when they no longer work.

CONSIDER THIS:

What rules are you following that limit closeness in your relationships?

What is the origin of some of the rules you developed for yourself in relationships with others?

● ● ●

W hen you are unclear, you give people the power to make decisions for you. They will take liberties and do what works for them, but that may not be what works for you.

Clear communication is twofold; it can get you what you want and set expectations for others.

Possible reasons you might fear being clear:

- **The other person's feelings might get hurt.** *Yes, this is possible. Meanwhile, your feelings are hurt because you aren't getting what you want.*

- **The other person might respond in a way that makes you feel uncomfortable.** *This is likely true, but you are already feeling uncomfortable. Hence, you are considering having a tough conversation.*

- **The relationship might end because the other person can't handle your truth.** *It rarely happens, but it is certainly possible. Dealing with incongruent needs in a relationship can be a sad but necessary act.*

● ● ●

Pinterest had a hold on me for a while. I would see a craft on the site, save it, purchase items to make it, and never complete the project. While packing to move, I discovered totes of crafting supplies that I had never used.

Sometimes, we must simply use what we already have.

Before you buy more or seek something new, ask yourself:

▸ *Do I have a free resource to help me with this?*

▸ *Has something I've already done solved this problem?*

● ● ●

You can feel conflicted even when you've made a healthy choice.

Right and wrong choices are sometimes revealed by the impact of our actions. If you decide to move to a new city for a promising job and everything works out, it might feel like a good choice. If you decide to move to a new city for a promising job but hate the job, it might feel like a bad choice. Success is never a guarantee.

Feeling conflicted is a healthy sign that you care about doing the right thing.

• • •

W hat seems easy is often not easy at all.

My artist friend helped me create a unique piece for my niece. During her instruction, I heard her uttering, "It's easy; just do this . . ." It wasn't easy at all for me. It was easy for her because of her gifts and years of practice. When visiting museums, abstract pieces seem easy to create independently, but we must remember that artists have skills.

People who make things appear easy have spent time perfecting their skills. You start as a beginner, not an expert. Learn at your own pace.

Before you tell someone "It's easy," remember the time and effort you put into acquiring the skill you now consider simple.

Yes, you may be a natural at something, making it easy from the beginning. But most tasks are hard at first and only become easy with time.

● ● ●

As a student of self-care in the 1990s and early 2000s, I saw a lot of information that relayed the message that "forgiveness is not about the other person; it's about you." Forgiveness was presented as something we *have* to do. In recent years, however, there's been a shift in that thinking.

Forgiveness is always a choice. We cannot make people forgive. What I have seen clinically is that it is more important to let go of the anger associated with the harm that was done than it is to forgive.

Forgiveness can look like no longer holding a grudge, feeling less angry, or being able to move forward. But this doesn't necessarily mean that we keep the person who harmed us in our life.

Forgiveness can happen without apologies, because we decide to accept what happened and learn to live with it.

Forgiveness is not a path to tolerating similar behaviors in the future.

Forgiveness does not guarantee we'll feel better about what happened but ensures that we learn to accept it.

Forgiveness doesn't need to happen within a specific time frame. When we try to force ourselves to forgive quickly, we may later feel resentment and wonder why.

● ● ●

S tay on your side of the street.

Visiting botanical gardens is one of my favorite pastimes. Large gardens require lots of care and attention. Instead of trying to increase the size of my own garden, I'm satisfied with admiring the lush escapes of the beautiful gardens across the nation.

Sometimes, the lives of others can seem so attractive that you'll start to believe you are supposed to do the same thing. You will know it's wrong for you, however, when you do it and immediately find yourself feeling dissatisfied.

Find where you have talents, and go after what you enjoy. Don't buy into the idea that to be satisfied, you must do or have what others do or have. Rather than mimic others, find what is unique to you.

●　●　●

Many of us get hung up on being perceived as lazy. I think we judge ourselves as lazy when we believe there are things we should be doing besides resting or taking it easy. But really, "laziness" is a term that we alone define. There's no universal list of behaviors that we could all agree are lazy.

There are times when we choose not to do what we *should* be doing, but when we decide to rest, that is not laziness. Just because we are not hyperproductive doesn't mean we're lazy.

The less busy we are, the more time we have to pursue or discover what matters.

If we want ease, we have to create it with the same level of commitment we reserve for being productive.

Less focus on productivity means more focus on creating a peaceful existence with less pressure.

Here are a few ways to be less productive:

▸ *Get lost in fiction.*

▸ *Work out to music instead of listening to podcasts.*

▸ *Create something for yourself without monetizing it.*

Laziness is the extreme of doing nothing. Discover the harmony of doing what needs to be done but also knowing when you've done enough.

● ● ●

A nxiety, depression, bipolar disorder, attention deficit hyperactivity disorder (ADHD), and other mental health issues are not a choice.

They are conditions that people would choose not to have if they had the option. Snapping out of it, choosing to be happy, or just feeling better are not realistic solutions to mental health issues.

Positive affirmations, going for walks, or just "getting over it" are overprescribed. Mental health issues have depth and are far too complicated to release with a few meditation videos.

You are not failing if simple solutions haven't worked for you. Clients new to therapy often wonder, "How long will this take?" The answer is complicated and without guarantees. I can promise that it will take time, and time moves faster when you're patient with yourself.

Beware of any information that claims to deliver a quick fix to a complicated problem.

CONSIDER THIS:

Everyone has mental health issues to some extent, but not everyone experiences mental health issues at a clinical (diagnosable) level.

Use social media and the internet as information, but get a formal diagnosis from a mental health professional.

Quick fixes will not resolve years of untreated issues.

● ● ●

After becoming a "social media figure," I still struggle to find a term that feels right for me, as this was hardly an occupational consideration twenty years ago. In 2017, I told friends of my goal to become a mental health figure with major assistance from building a community on social media. In hindsight, it sounds audacious, since it hadn't been done and isn't easy to achieve. Despite skepticism from a few, I continued on my journey and achieved my goal within a few years. The skeptics are now impressed that my big dream was actually realized.

It's normal to want people to affirm your dreams, because it gives you a sense of connection. However, people will sometimes be discouraging even though your goal could be excellent for you.

Many things sound wild and impossible before they become reality. Many modern conveniences we rely on every day were once a pipe dream until someone believed in them enough to pursue creating them. Sometimes, we don't know what's possible until we make it happen.

Pursue your dreams even when the support for them is low. Anyone who has been the first to pursue something has dealt with others doubting them along the way.

● ● ●

The brain is busy creating stories. Notice when you're adding more details to the story than what exists.

Madeline believed her father, James, didn't love her mother because he remarried within a year after her mother's death. James had been married to Madeline's mother for thirty-two years, and he grieved the loss of companionship. Then, he found himself growing closer to a neighbor who was also a widow.

Madeline made up a story about her father's feelings that wasn't true.

Common narratives we might create that aren't helpful:

▸ *"Nobody likes me."*

▸ *"I always mess up."*

▸ *"I'll never find a partner for a serious relationship."*

When this happens with my clients, I catch them and say, "Now, that's a great screenplay." It's not real; it's fiction.

CONSIDER THIS:

Are there underlying themes that contribute to a particular story? For example: "I have to be a good girl."

Is the story based in reality?

What are its origins?

Your life becomes a reflection of your stories, so be mindful of the truth.

● ● ●

You deserve to be loved when you're still learning to love yourself. A lack of self-love doesn't mean that you shouldn't be loved by others.

You can receive love while learning how to love yourself.

People can love you with your imperfections. Release the belief that you can't be loved until you love yourself.

Humans deserve love no matter how they feel about themselves.

● ● ●

L abels can mean different things to people, so define your terms. For example, your version of love or commitment might not be the same as someone else's. What do the terms mean for you and the other person in the relationship?

PRACTICE THIS:

When I say **love,** *I mean* _____.

When I say **commitment,** *I mean* _____.

When I say **girlfriend,** *I mean* _____.

When I say **father,** *I mean* _____.

When we assume that others are following our definitions, we are likely wrong.

Your lack of definition could be impacting your relationships.

● ● ●

O thers who appear very different from you are not necessarily that different internally.

When Halle Berry was a guest on *The Oprah Winfrey Show*, she talked about her insecurities around beauty. To many, she is a beautiful woman, but she didn't believe it about herself.

When you become jealous of others or place people on pedestals, it's easy to forget that they are imperfect. Humans experience insecurities, heartbreaks, traumas, perfectionist tendencies, and many other issues despite how they may present themselves. Empathy helps us see each other's wholeness, not just the highlights.

In the stories you create about others, don't forget to be empathetic.

● ● ●

W e've all been getting older since birth. The one-year-old is older than the one-day-old.

Notice aging, and remember it's been happening all along. It isn't just for "old people" or others. It's a reality for all of us, every day.

• • •

V acations aren't magic. They simply give you a break from the chaos, burnout, or whatever you're trying to escape. But you will return to what you left.

When you need an escape, only to return to chaos, challenge yourself to fix the mess.

▸ *In your everyday life, what do you want to vacate (be honest)?*

▸ *Could you develop a new perspective about what you can't change?*

▸ *Is there a different way to respond to what you can't change?*

▸ *Where do you need more support?*

▸ *In what areas do you need to do less?*

▸ *How can you incorporate some of the things you love about vacation into your daily life?*

Vacations are not a solution to a life that doesn't have boundaries and peace.

● ● ●

If I always do everything my way, it leaves little space for me to learn how to do things in a new way.

If everyone around me thinks like me, I only see one viewpoint.

Thinking like me is just one way, not the only way.

Of course, in practice, it can be hard to accept our differences with others.

But expecting people to be just like us is a recipe for disappointment. Assuming people have the same abilities, desires, or preferences leaves little room for individuality.

"If it were me, I would . . ." is a phrase often used to imply that others should do as you do.

A "my way is best" or "my way is the only way" type of thinking does not build connection with others. It breeds conflict and resentment.

We are similar and not the same.

Different paths can lead to good outcomes.

Diversity is about being open to differences even when they are not familiar to you.

● ● ●

L ife is short.

Ninety-nine years isn't even long enough when most of the time is spent waiting on others to start.

Instead, make the first move.

Tell people how much they matter to you, and show them you care.

Waiting for others to do it first is a missed opportunity for connection.

Sure, it's understandable to want to protect your feelings. But if you avoid everything that's potentially harmful, you won't ever take a risk.

Love is both risky and rewarding.

Life is too short to miss out on love because you fear it won't be returned. Keep risking and find out.

● ● ●

Coddling people after you set boundaries is a form of people-pleasing.

Affirmations:

▸ *I don't have to soften the blow or lessen the impact.*

▸ *It's not within my power to determine how people will respond to information.*

▸ *I can have boundaries even when the other person is likely to be upset.*

▸ *Some boundaries aren't pleasant.*

People can dislike your boundaries and learn to respect them.

Give people time to feel what they need to feel. Your boundaries may be shocking to the other person even though they feel like common sense to you.

In some cases, it may be unreasonable to expect others to be happy with your boundaries. After all, you're setting boundaries because what you wanted wasn't happening naturally.

It takes time to adjust to change. Let people adjust, but don't ease up on your boundaries just to appease them.

● ● ●

My children are of the era of giving everyone in their class a Valentine's Day card. At my urban public school growing up, we only gave Valentine's cards to our friends. Unfortunately, some children were awakened to how many friends they did or didn't have. The current way is kinder. Not everyone is going to be our friend, but we can show them basic respect nonetheless.

You don't have to like everyone. Essentially, this means you don't have to build relationships with people who are not your cup of tea.

It's better to be kind to someone even if you don't like them than it is to force yourself to build a relationship with someone you dislike. Kindness simply means treating people with respect and dignity.

Conversely, being kind to people you don't like is not the same as showering people with kindness when they are mean to you. If someone has demonstrated a lack of respect for you, it could be a kindness to yourself to limit your engagement with them, if possible.

Whether you like someone or not, disrespect is never okay.

● ● ●

The loudest and most influential voice in your head is your own.

Radical self-kindness is how you learn to love yourself despite not always getting it right.

With practice (sometimes lots of practice), you can learn to speak kindly to yourself. Ask "What would I say to a friend?" or "What would I say to a child?" This might help you develop the skills of talking more softly to yourself. When you are mean to yourself, it reflects in your decision-making.

Kind statements that could help:

▸ *You are not bad; you made an unwise decision.*

▸ *You aren't dumb; you didn't know.*

▸ *You repeated the same mistake because you're hopeful.*

Speak to yourself as if you're the most precious person on the planet . . . because you are.

● ● ●

Being a nice person doesn't mean lowering your standards. Accepting less than what you want is unkind to yourself.

Nice people can have expectations—and walk away if they're not met.

• • •

If the shoe doesn't fit, don't wear it.

Sometimes, we force ourselves to be like others.

You don't have to be a morning person, meditate, or journal daily to have a harmonious life. Create a pace that you can follow. Adopt enjoyable habits, not forced ones. There are so many wellness practices, so choose the ones that work for you.

You will not enjoy journaling if you hate journaling.

You will not like meditation if it bores you.

You will not like cold showers if they cause you more stress.

You don't need to practice everything. Pursue what works for you.

● ● ●

Creating makes you creative. Be an audience of one.

Whatever you love to create, do it for your own satisfaction. Creating art, writing, styling, etc., happens by doing—with or without an audience of spectators.

When you create to perform, you might be less authentic. Trying to create just for others may leave you with a scattered vision. Some people will want more color, while others will want less. You can't do both. So enjoy what you create for yourself.

Of course, you might want someone else to enjoy your work. But if you create what's meaningful to you, the right people will follow. And even if you don't create for public consumption, you're still a creative person.

● ● ●

B uild community. You cannot get everything you need from one person, and it exhausts people to be a singular source of support.

Seek collective support to ensure that everything is not weighted on one or a few individuals.

• • •

When we assume people know the reasons behind their actions, we assume they are self-aware. But not everyone is willing to self-reflect. Some people act without insight or assessment.

Before saying "Why did they do that?" or "They should know better," remember that some people lack the insight to understand themselves.

Introspection requires courage, because it means we might see something about ourselves that we don't like. When someone refuses introspection, it leaves them with nothing to correct. A lack of self-awareness allows many people to continue existing as they are—and this prevents them from taking responsibility for the chaos in their relationships.

People see what they want when they are ready.

● ● ●

A friend sees me as a master at manifestation. She notices how I take immediate action toward what I say I want.

However, manifesting is merely dreaming until you add action.

Putting words to what you want is step one. Working toward your goals is the critical ingredient.

Manifesting is not magic; it's action.

●　●　●

When I lived in Detroit, my sense of security was low while my defenses were high. One day at an open market called Eastern Market, I purchased too many flowers to carry to my car at once. When an older man picked up my pot of flowers and started carrying them in the direction of my car, I got anxious and shouted, "Where are you going with my flowers?"

"I was helping you to your car," he responded. To my nervous system, his help felt like robbery.

Reconsider the stories you tell yourself about how you've been wronged.

Sometimes, your suspicions are true, but other times they are just a result of your past experiences. What are the facts, and what are you assuming? If every story ends with your being wronged, perhaps it's time to take a look at the storyteller.

More than one side exists, and considering the other person's perspective is valuable for growth. It isn't always them; sometimes, it's you or both of you.

● ● ●

E asy isn't the way to success.

I remember learning how to read, and it wasn't easy.

I remember starting at a new school and adjusting to a new environment, and it wasn't easy.

I remember learning lots of complicated things. Sometimes, I felt anxious or even defeated, but in the end, I was proud that I kept going.

When you expect something to be easy, recall some of the hard things you've mastered in the past, like learning to write, riding a bike, or speaking in front of others.

You have tried so many things and succeeded—remember that.

▸ *What are you quitting too soon?*

▸ *What do you need to give yourself more time to practice?*

▸ *Did you give up on something that you might return to?*

● ● ●

Drew thought she was a "nice person." She was actually "faux nice." She smiled in the face of others but talked negatively about them behind their backs. She wanted people to perceive her as nice in their presence, but she wasn't truly a nice person.

You are what you do, not who you think you are.

Sometimes, we identify ourselves as one type of person and behave outwardly like another. You may see yourself differently from how others see you. After all, your description of yourself has a lot to do with what you think of yourself, not what you actually do.

It's possible to be congruent in your thoughts and actions by being honest about what you do every day.

CONSIDER THIS:

Who are you really?

What do others say about who you are?

Which of your behaviors don't fit with who you want to be?

● ● ●

You don't have to be the best at something to enjoy it. Writing, dancing, painting, singing, and so much more can be done for joy.

Start doing things for fun, whether you ever master them or not.

• • •

L et others have their opinions about you.

People are free to have opinions, and you are free to disagree with them. When you try to prove people wrong, you seek their approval. Live your life knowing that you don't have to change someone else's opinion about you.

My inbox is overrun with people lamenting about how others have the wrong impression of them:

▶ *"My sister-in-law spreads lies about me to other family members."*

▶ *"My friend told our friend group something private about my sex life, and now everyone has an opinion about my private life."*

You can't make people see you as you would like. People are free to form their own opinions, whether their opinions are fact, fiction, or a mixture of both.

●　●　●

S pend more time doing what you love" is a common saying. But how do you actually start this practice when your life has been filled with tasks you feel you *have* to do whether you enjoy them or not?

▸ *You must first create space to explore what you love. Space is there, but you're filling it with everything else. Eliminate and downsize to start discovering more.*

▸ *Notice what exhausts and depletes you.*

▸ *Pour energy into valuable relationships.*

▸ *Clear the mental clutter about what you think you* should *be doing and focus more on what you love to do.*

▸ *Find a rhythm that works for you, and don't try to keep up with anyone else's pace.*

▸ *Get to know yourself more deeply, because self-knowledge reveals what you enjoy.*

Of course, this doesn't mean abandoning everything you don't like to do. You will need to do those things, too, and you don't have to love them. But it's easier to do those less enjoyable tasks when they are part of a fuller life with time devoted to fun and joy as well.

● ● ●

Did someone tell you how you should feel or what feelings supposedly make sense, while other feelings do not?

Feelings don't have to make sense to other people for them to be true for you.

Sometimes, we are conflicted about our emotions because we try to justify them.

But our feelings don't have to be understandable.

Feel what you feel without trying to make it logical. Feelings are complicated, and sometimes there is no discernible reason for them. They just are.

● ● ●

When major events happen in the world, the news cycle is centered on hypotheses about what happened and what caused it. Factual reporting takes time, but speculating captures viewers more than saying "We don't have much information yet" does.

In our personal lives, as well, thinking we know the truth is not the same as knowing the truth.

When we "think" we know something, it's often based on assumptions, while actual knowledge is based on facts.

Ensure your information is rooted in facts, not assumptions. If you need more clarity, ask questions and wait until you can discover the truth.

We create relationship issues when we act on assumptions.

Clarity saves relationships and minimizes disputes.

● ● ●

O ffer grace.

When someone has done something wrong, it's usually unhelpful to say "You messed up" or "Why didn't you think before you acted?" It's more helpful to share how you've made similar mistakes. Try to see the situation from the other person's point of view. It was an accident even if it was an unwise one.

Shaming people will not encourage them to change. Letting someone know it's okay to make a mistake gives them the courage to try again. Recipes are perfected, for example, after many failed attempts.

In the film *Almost Christmas*, the character played by Danny Glover (no relation) tries over and over to re-create the sweet potato pie recipe of his late wife. Finally, after many comically disgusting failures, he finds the perfect ingredients.

Hopefully, you will learn to make different mistakes and not repeat the same ones you've made before.

● ● ●

Notice when you choose peace, chaos, or confusion. If you say you don't like drama, what choices are you making to support a drama-free life?

Are your actions congruent with your desires?

If you are still running toward situations you'd rather not experience, be honest with yourself:

▸ *Perhaps there's a part of you that enjoys a little drama.*

▸ *Perhaps you don't have the tools to live differently.*

▸ *Perhaps you're afraid to change.*

▸ *Perhaps you feel comfortable with drama because it's familiar.*

▸ *Perhaps you're unaware that you're the common factor in all of the situations you face.*

Repeat After Me:

Peace is my goal.

● ● ●

Passive communication seems safe. The other person isn't inconvenienced or uncomfortable, so they remain pleased with you. But over time, silence leads to resentment in relationships. When counseling couples on the verge of divorce, I often hear "I didn't want to hurt their feelings."

In most instances, it would have been more beneficial to be assertive than to avoid the problem. The temporary discomfort of telling the truth leads to long-term satisfaction in our relationships.

Remember, silence is not a healthy comfort zone.

● ● ●

My work as a therapist has taught me that there's only so much helping or assisting that I can do in a single day. Some days, I jump right into work. I like to see my clients back to back, so on a given day I may have seven or eight clients. When I get off work, I don't always have it in me to talk to a person who's a chronic complainer. Even if my clients didn't complain, I may just be at capacity for problem-solving. It doesn't mean that I never want to talk to that person again; it just means that on this particular day, I'm tapped out.

Some signs that you may be at or over capacity include:

▸ *You feel like you will lose it if just one more thing happens.*

▸ *You don't feel like yourself.*

▸ *You feel tired and can't figure out why.*

▸ *You're not interested in your usual routine.*

▸ *You feel like you're "over" people.*

▸ *You feel irritable.*

▸ *You find it hard to listen to others.*

▸ *You indulge in your vices more than usual.*

It is better to acknowledge when you're at capacity than to do a poor job because you've taken on too much. We have to take care of ourselves and be honest with ourselves about whether we are in a space to be of service to others.

Taking on more than you're equipped to handle can backfire.

● ● ●

Jeffrey thought he was ready to go back to work just one month after his father passed away. However, on most days he found himself crying in the bathroom. He was tired of feeling sad and ready to move on with his life, but his grief still needed to be felt, even if it was inconvenient for him.

CONSIDER THIS:

What are you trying not to see?

What are you trying not to feel?

Perhaps the solution is allowing the thoughts and feelings to be there, exploring them, and taking action toward healing. Ignoring them is not a way forward.

● ● ●

Acquaintances and friends are different types of relationships, and you can't expect the same from both. Acquaintances can fulfill a need for a surface-level connection, and sometimes, they evolve into friends.

Friendships are deep connections that are mutual. In friendships, there are expectations and commonalities that keep the relationship flourishing. What you disclose in a friendship might be different from what you disclose in a relationship with an acquaintance.

Sometimes, we get mad at acquaintances for not acting like friends, but when we recognize the difference between the two, our expectations are more realistic.

●　●　●

N ot every situation is a learning experience. When we learn a lesson from an experience, we feel we can prevent a similar situation in the future. But sometimes, problems can't be prevented.

The other day, I hurt my leg doing something routine while traveling. No lessons were learned to help me avoid a similar injury in the future. I was already being careful, so there was nothing more I could have done.

● ● ●

J ulie said, "I don't speak up, because no one listens to me."

When you feel people won't listen to you, repeat yourself, rephrase your need, or share your concern with someone who can help. Try again (and again) before quitting. Make an effort to be understood.

If someone refuses to hear you, does the relationship align with your needs?

● ● ●

Accept that even on your best days, you will not be amazing to everyone. Even when you have the best intentions, people will be mad at you or annoyed by you.

People will say untrue things about you.

Someone will be hurt by something you did.

You can't manage how people feel about you.

You can manage how you respond to how people feel about you. If you try to control how they feel, however, you might be inauthentic to try to sway them.

Discomfort is needed for growth. Authenticity is required for connection.

CONSIDER THIS:

Who is someone whom others are fond of but you aren't?

Recall a time when you annoyed someone. How did/does that impact your behaviors with others?

● ● ●

Independence and self-reliance often lead us to do things without support. Sure, you can paint a room by yourself. But with a few friends, it might be more enjoyable, and time will pass more easily. When you become known as the type of person who needs little support from others, people might not offer. Therefore, you will need to ask.

CONSIDER THIS:

Do others know when you need them?

Are you attempting to manage everything on your own?

● ● ●

D on't overthink it" is a difficult direction to follow when you're in a cycle of ruminating thoughts. A symptom of anxiety is the inability to stop overthinking.

Instead of trying to stop your thoughts, welcome them. Examine their meaning. Consider their root cause, and devise a solution. Allowing your thoughts is more helpful than wishing them away or trying to distract yourself. Our current culture seems to imply that distractions such as alcohol, social media, risky sex, etc., will alleviate troubling thoughts. But the thoughts are still there after the distraction is over. Confronting, allowing, and being with your thoughts is intentionally helpful and may allow you to gain clarity about what you need.

● ● ●

G racefully accept compliments.

It's okay if this makes you feel uncomfortable. Hold back when you want to dispute the positive words someone has said.

Allowing compliments to flow invites more kindness into your life.

Practice Saying This:

*Thank you so much for your kind words.
It means a lot to me that you think so highly of me.*

Hopefully, one day you'll believe the wonderful things people say about you.

● ● ●

Recommitment is as significant as the initial commitment.

You will stumble, shift, or have moments of inconsistency that require recommitment. Refuse to give up on starting over. With gardening, when one seed doesn't grow, you plant another one.

If you haven't reached out to a friend in a month, don't let it turn into two months—connect with them today.

If you vowed to go to bed without scrolling social media but you scrolled last night, put your phone down tonight.

Recommitment can mean renewing your vows to yourself. Renew your self-commitments over and over. Take everything day by day, moment by moment.

Resist the urge to stick to what you don't want. This will creep in as "I can't" language:

▸ *"I can't put my phone down."*

▸ *"I can't go for a walk."*

Be a person who starts over often.

● ● ●

Thoughts and actions must align for change to happen.

People who find it hard to do better struggle to align their thoughts with actions. Deciding to change is a wavering process filled with transitions and restarts. It's possible, but it isn't easy.

Change offers possibilities, while staying stuck gives you more of the same.

You change when you feel ready or when you are most impacted by staying the same.

CONSIDER THIS:

What needs to change in your life?

What could stand to change, but you aren't ready to act on?

• • •

P eople tell you who you are, and sometimes you need to
believe them.

When someone you trust says something about you, don't dismiss
it just because it isn't what you want to believe about yourself.
Hear them out.

People can experience you in ways that you disagree with,
but it can be an accurate depiction of who you are.

People will be honest with you when you demonstrate you
can listen.

People will be dishonest with you when you demonstrate
you can't handle criticism.

● ● ●

Perhaps you don't need to be your old self again. The past was nice, but there could be something better in store.

Be willing to reinvent yourself or create something right where you are. Copying the old version stifles growth and doesn't leave room for your current life.

For example, the old me could eat an entire bag of Flamin' Hot Cheetos without having stomach pains, but I can't do that anymore.

I can no longer listen to people tell lies about themselves and pretend to believe them to boost their ego, but the old me could.

You can miss who you were without revisiting the past. Evolve into someone new.

• • •

I t's okay to pause while healing.

Humanness involves issues to work through, explore, and fix. But there's no reward for the fastest healer.

Slow down when needed. Pause and return. Shift your focus to a different area. Pausing is not the same as abandoning. Recognize when you need a break, and be brave enough to step back.

Healing can take many forms, and it's an ongoing practice.

Move at your own pace.

● ● ●

A personal issue may actually be a mental health issue. Due to a lack of understanding, people sometimes assume that others can change swiftly by using willpower to alleviate anxiety, depression, addiction, and other problems.

When evaluating the behaviors of others, consider their mental health, and strive to be more empathetic. Everyone has mental health issues, but we're impacted at varying levels.

When you're affected by someone's mental health issues, remember that it isn't personal; it's mental health.

Depression, anger, having a bad day, or any other reason is not an excuse to mistreat others, however. If you are unhealed, going through something, or not at your best, it's your job to manage your behaviors toward others.

● ● ●

W hat you want for others may not be what they want for themselves.

You can love people, but you cannot save them.

You can love people, but you can't think for them.

You can love people but cause them harm by preventing them from figuring out their own solutions.

It can be hard to watch someone do something you don't agree with or something that might harm them. But adults have the freedom to choose.

Help without meddling.

Help without giving so much that you lose yourself.

Help in ways that allow you to be present but not consumed.

Healthy boundaries should be activated when you help others.

● ● ●

Discomfort is a growth tool.

You can build confidence when you try big experiences (and sometimes even small ones) that you find scary. You become more potent when you're willing to be uncomfortable now for the promise of later success.

It's possible, however, to be too risky or not risky enough. The sweet spot is moving toward experiences that are worth the risk to you.

"It's not easy" equals "I don't want to be uncomfortable." Increase your risk tolerance as a path to creating a more fulfilling life.

Try this affirmation:

Moments of discomfort are part of evolving.

CONSIDER THIS:

What's worth experiencing discomfort for?

● ● ●

When you lack appropriate education about mental health, you might assume that if a person does X, they might feel better. Bear in mind that feeling depressed is different from being diagnosed with depression. Feeling anxious is different from being diagnosed with panic disorder.

A disorder means that the issue is severe enough that it affects the person's ability to function. Even those who are underdiagnosed or diagnosed without treatment are impacted daily by their mental health issues.

Resources are scarce for those who need them most. Sometimes, the only solution people know is to negatively self-medicate, stay the same, or do just enough to get by. Mental health care is improving but not fast enough for everyone to receive adequate and dignified care.

So before you judge, consider how challenging it might be for someone to admit they don't have the tools, they need help, or they need to learn how to implement new skills, sometimes in unsupportive environments.

● ● ●

In relationships of all kinds, what you do for others is often a reflection of your own needs. When you're unclear about your needs, notice what feels natural to do for others.

Do you love to listen? Perhaps you'd like to be heard.

Do you like giving people thoughtful gifts? Perhaps you like receiving gifts.

Your deeds toward others can be a mirror of your own expectations. In relationships, it can be helpful to note if you are honoring the needs of others or projecting your needs onto them.

You may start to resent people when they don't appreciate your efforts. But is it what they asked for? Pay attention to what people truly want. Doing things that matter to you but not to the other person will frustrate both of you.

People may feel neglected when you're not giving them what they really want or need. People are unique, so what one person needs may not be the same as what another does.

●　●　●

U nreasonable expectations destroy relationships. To decide if an expectation is unreasonable, consider the other person. Have they demonstrated the ability to meet the expectation? Is it something you assume everyone should be capable of?

Also consider the source of the expectation. Are you requesting something that's rooted in an unmet need from past relationships? For instance, my parents always seemed too busy to spend time with me. Therefore, I want my partner to shower me with attention.

Expectations are essential for your well-being, but sometimes, we create expectations that are impossible for others to meet.

● ● ●

Categorizing and labeling don't define every part of you or anyone else. Labels can help you connect and find community, but they can also box you in.

Pay attention to when labels make you rigid, judgmental, or pushy. Labels should enhance your understanding, not close your mind to other possibilities.

Find a label that fits, and be open to shifting it or not using it to sum up all parts of you or anyone else.

● ● ●

On an episode of the podcast *Other People's Lives*, a guest talks about overspending on sneakers. Despite having financial issues, the guest used these purchases as a way of restoring her ego after being bullied in childhood for having cheap, off-brand shoes. But having hundreds of pairs of shoes and being in debt didn't resolve the pain of being bullied. An emotional void cannot be filled with stuff. You cannot buy your way out of sadness, but you can dig yourself deeper into other issues in the process.

In a culture of more, more, more, we've made contentment seem negative.

Contentment is peaceful and offers you rest. The search for more, on the other hand, means you never reach "enough," because the target is always moving.

Discover the peaceful harmony between wanting more and being satisfied where you are at the same time.

CONSIDER THIS:

What will enough look like for you?

What will you do once you reach "enough"?

What voids are you trying to fill with stuff?

● ● ●

Grieving in advance of loss doesn't stop you from suffering when the loss happens. Perhaps there is some comfort in managing your emotions when you have a warning. However, you cannot prevent feelings that need to flow.

When you stop yourself from getting too excited about something, it's a way to control your grief if it doesn't work out.

Keep your hopes high. You deserve to wish for big things, impossible things, and miracles.

There is no such thing as preventing sadness by grieving in advance.

● ● ●

Distance is sometimes healthy. Perhaps we want to keep a relationship without engaging with someone on a regular basis. Every relationship is not an everyday relationship, and some relationships are annual, monthly, or biweekly, just like a subscription. We are allowed to decide what we want and what works best for us, even if the other person is demanding more.

Sometimes the break leads to the recognition that there is something beyond repair, but other times, it's just a break. It's taking a breath. We get to decide what that distance means. The goal of the break is to take the time you need to be able to approach the relationship in a way that is more intentional, with a fresh mindset and new strategies for engaging with that person.

Some of the reasons you may find yourself needing to take a break are as follows:

- *You notice that your energy is impacted by interactions with the person.*

- *You notice that you become easily frustrated or short-tempered while or after being around them.*

- *You feel that your boundaries aren't honored.*

- *You don't feel comfortable being yourself around this person.*

- *You're in a different season of your life. As our priorities and interests shift, our people may shift as well. If you are really into plants, you may want to be around a bunch of plant people. Likewise, if all your friends are going through divorces and you're trying to figure out how to make your marriage work, you may not want to be in that space. It's okay to center your needs and take a pause.*

● ● ●

Our lives are full of gentle endings. Think about the number of people you've met in life, even from one grade to another when you were in elementary school. Your friends changed from year to year and often with very little fanfare. There wasn't a conversation about it. You just split. This kind of easeful separation is possible even in adulthood.

You may not want to end a relationship, but you might want to spend less time with the person.

TRY THIS:

Step back slowly.

Observe your habits around reaching out.

Be honest.

Be clear that it's about you and not the other person.

Express how much you care about them, and let them know this is a way you're caring for yourself.

Decide if the relationship can be repaired.

You know you no longer enjoy someone's company when interacting feels like a chore or when it's a reaction to habit, not desire.

● ● ●

J ustin was clear he didn't want to have children. Whenever he mentioned it to his mother, she said that he'd regret his decision and that his life would be lonely without kids. She never convinced him to have children, but it certainly made him uncomfortable with sharing other life decisions with her.

Be mindful of when you try to persuade someone to be like you.

Pause and try to understand why you're trying to convince others.

Are you seeking validation for your life choices?

Are they challenging your values?

Is something harmful happening?

Telling others what they "should" do or offering unsolicited advice is an indication that you're trying to get everyone on the same team.

You can know a lot and still not know what is best for others. Mind your business when others make life choices. Everyone wants the freedom to decide for themselves.

REMEMBER THIS:

Your way is one way but not the only way.

● ● ●

E nvironment impacts your mental health.

Sometimes, your environment is an unsafe neighborhood, a negative friend group, a highly competitive work environment, or a challenging home life. Being surrounded by anything that's unhealthy for you will affect you physically, emotionally, and mentally. You may find yourself adapting by becoming more like your environment or escaping mentally to be able to function.

CONSIDER THIS:

What in your environment is impacting your mental health?

How do you cope when you can't control your environment?

What's in your control to change?

• • •

N ot caring is unhealthy.

People say "I don't want to care about it anymore." This is a way to protect yourself from feeling any discomfort.

Not caring is avoidance. Not caring is apathetic.

Perhaps you can care and learn to deal with the discomfort.

Perhaps you can care and respond differently.

Perhaps you can care and not become undone.

Caring is a healthy part of the human experience. Care, and learn to soothe yourself in healthy ways.

● ● ●

When more than one relationship ends for a similar reason, it's a pattern. Even when you see others as the problem, remember that you invited them to occupy space in your life.

Lisa's romantic relationships moved fast, were instantly deep, and ended in high drama. Typically, she noted that the other person was the cause of the relationship failure, and she had no choice but to end it abruptly. Sometimes, we choose the same thing because we overlook our role in the pattern.

Unwanted patterns will repeat until we create new patterns by unlearning unhealthy beliefs. We must commit to establishing new beliefs in order to change our patterns.

● ● ●

S ticks and stones may break my bones, but words can never hurt me."

I've never been hit with a stick or stone, but harsh statements have stuck with me. Words hurt.

Speak your mind, but consider your words before speaking. Be mindful of your tone. The goal is to communicate effectively, not to destroy or attack.

Aggressive language turns hard conversations into battlefields.

People remember what you said, even when you didn't mean it. There is no unhearing what was said.

● ● ●

Relationships are not a sport.

Defensiveness seems like protection, but it can be a barrier.

If you are uncorrectable, you refuse to incorporate new ideas.

If you are blocking others out, your only perspective is your own.

If no one can be honest with you, everyone has to hold back.

Do you want authentic relationships or ones where you're perceived as doing no wrong?

When you struggle with defensiveness, as many of us do from time to time, repeat this:

▸ *"I'm not on a battlefield. I'm having a conversation."*

▸ *"This might be hard to hear, but it can be helpful."*

▸ *"I can explore what's being said without having to agree with it."*

▸ *"Even if I'm criticized, I am not a bad person."*

TRY THIS:

Take a deep breath, and remember that honest (healthy) feedback fosters growth.

Acknowledge your defensiveness, and listen.

Ask questions centered on understanding, not defending.

● ● ●

C lear values determine your steps and your boundaries.

Lack of clarity can lead you to try a lot of things that aren't aligned with what you value. You might focus on what looks good to others or what you think you *should* do.

Clarity about your values creates vision, alignment, and ease.

When you determine your values, you'll know more about what you can, will, and won't do.

▸ *What are you moving toward?*

● ● ●

W hat is meant for you will feel natural, not forced. It is a knowing that "this is where I'm supposed to be" or "this is what I'm supposed to be doing."

When you want something to work that isn't natural for you, you will try to make it fit when it doesn't. For instance, double-booking your schedule is a sign that you're forcing what doesn't fit.

Force is a sign that you're on the wrong path.

If the key doesn't fit, you're at the wrong door.

If the path is not clear, perhaps you're on the wrong trail.

●　●　●

Our most profound work is understanding and accepting who we are.

It can be hard to be yourself when who you are hasn't been enough for others. Remember, they were trying to make you like them instead of embracing you.

Of course, there are things you may want to change about yourself. But be clear about the reason for your changes.

▸ *Are you trying to be less yourself for them?*

▸ *Who is motivating your desire to change?*

Let any changes be self-driven and not because someone has told you that you aren't enough as you are.

● ● ●

Assertiveness and aggressiveness are often confused. Far too often, you may think you are "being honest," "telling it like it is," or "speaking the truth." To others, however, it's mean, unkind, and harmful.

Every thought doesn't have to be communicated. Some thoughts are for you to keep to yourself.

What you might consider a truth that needs to be shared could be unhelpful and cause harm to another person.

How you speak matters as much as what you're saying. It's healthy to be assertive but harmful to your relationships when you communicate aggressively. Learn the difference.

● ● ●

You are responsible for taking care of yourself.

No one can do the work for you.

No one is responsible for making you more consistent with taking care of yourself.

This can be hard to accept when you expect others to take care of you.

When you don't care for yourself, others are pressured to take on this task. If they don't meet your expectations, the relationship will suffer.

Hold yourself accountable. You are the one creating your life, not other people.

Others can support you, and you should seek support. That's healthy. But adults are responsible for taking care of themselves unless there is a physical or mental limitation that prohibits them from doing so.

●　●　●

Trying to be like others makes you less like you.

Remember who you were before the world shaped you into something else.

CONSIDER THIS:

What parts of yourself have you abandoned in order to pursue the acceptance of others?

What parts of yourself do you want to reclaim?

What were your hobbies ten, fifteen, or twenty years ago?

So much of who we are is erased to fit in.

So much of who we are is suppressed to make life easier for others.

Be inspired by others without taking on behaviors and traits that don't fit your uniqueness.

Always return to yourself—no more self-betrayal for others' acceptance.

● ● ●

E nvy becomes dangerous when you refuse to recognize it.

You might inadvertently say harmful words. Your behaviors might become passive-aggressive.

Other people will have things you want.

▸ *What have you done or said when you were envious of someone?*

▸ *What has someone done or said when they were envious of you?*

CONSIDER THIS:

What's something you envy about a friend?

What's something you envy about a family member?

What's something you envy about your partner/spouse?

What's something you envy about a stranger on the internet?

I envied a friend when they got a new car, and I couldn't afford anything close to it.

I envied a cousin who appeared to have a more stable childhood.

I envied my partner's ability to be more carefree than me.

I envied those lifestyle influencers who pack beautiful lunches for their children.

Acknowledge your feelings to yourself, and decide how you want to treat people you envy.

● ● ●

Your greatest life challenge is becoming more comfortable with who you are.

We often spend our time trying to be like someone else, being who others want us to be, or attempting to be what we think is best, such as an extrovert or a morning person.

Declare with me:

I am not _____.

I am _____.

I am not _____.

I am _____.

I am not _____.

I am _____.

When you find it hard to be a certain way, it might be that you have moved too far from your true self. In an attempt to be like others, you can change beyond recognition.

• • •

I t's hard to slow down in a world obsessed with speed and a culture obsessed with productivity.

Notice yourself moving fast, taking shortcuts, trying to save time, and rushing.

I am even moving away from hurried language like:

▸ *"I need to hurry up and call this person."*

▸ *"Let me do this real quick."*

▸ *"Let me ask you something real quick."*

▸ *"I'll do that in just a second."*

The goal is to finish with your spirit intact, not depleted.
It's a fact that something will delay you, things won't turn out perfectly every time, and you will mess up.

Some other ways slowing down is showing up for me are:

▸ *Taking on more easeful work projects and fewer work projects on the whole*

▸ *Spending more time with friends who fill me up*

▸ *Having joyful conversations*

▸ *Sitting outside on the porch*

▸ *Making sure I'm drinking enough water throughout the day*

▸ *Watching my tea brew*

▸ *Drinking my tea while it's still hot*

▸ *Watching plants grow*

▸ *Really watching my television shows rather than half watching them*

You have time to do it with ease.

● ● ●

J ust because you have a logical reason for why something happened, it doesn't guarantee you'll feel better.

Knowing *why* doesn't justify bad things happening.

Knowing *why* doesn't alleviate anger.

Knowing *why* won't change the situation.

Knowing *why* can be helpful, but it may not give you the solace you desire. Peace is more likely to come when you accept that you can't change what happened.

● ● ●

Relationships are a practice ground for honing your communication skills. Sometimes, the relationship doesn't need to end; you just need to practice a skill. For example, you may need to practice being up front, asking for space when needed, and being more open-minded.

Repairing is a critical component in relationships. If you don't learn to repair, you'll be in a continuous cycle of ending and starting new relationships.

Starting over won't resolve poor relationship skills. In new relationships, without the appropriate skills, you will eventually find yourself in familiar territory.

This in no way means that you must remain in hurtful relationships. Instead, notice when you're leaving repairable relationships without doing anything to save them.

● ● ●

S ometimes the problem is not that we don't have friends but that we've allowed our connections to dwindle.

If you are looking for ways to rekindle old friendships:

- *Remember what's important to them. Make a point of reaching out to them on their birthdays and other days of special significance.*

- *Don't be deterred by how much time you have spent apart or how long it's been since you've spoken.*

● ● ●

B e gentle with yourself when old hurts still bother you.

Forgetting isn't possible. It's more reasonable to expect that you can gradually feel less affected by it or no longer focus on it as much.

Some things will never be okay with your spirit, and it's fine to honor that truth. When you stop trying to forget, space opens up to heal the things that still trouble you. Allowing yourself to feel what's present nurtures your spirit.

● ● ●

"Disappointment" isn't included enough in our vocabulary of feelings. It's hoping for something and not getting it. Do you fear saying that you want something? Does it seem stronger not to expect what you want? We use "don't be hopeful" language to try to avoid disappointment.

"Don't be hopeful" language might sound like:

▸ *"Don't get your hopes up."*

▸ *"I don't want to fail."*

▸ *"If I stop thinking about it, I won't care."*

But you can't avoid feeling disappointed. It's constructive to acknowledge when you feel it.

● ● ●

One way to manage passive-aggressiveness is to be vulnerable and honest about what bothers you.

Not wanting others to know you're bothered doesn't mean you aren't bothered. It means you're pretending.

Most people care, and brave people admit when they care.

A few phrases to help you get started:

I am upset because _____.

It hurt me when _____.

I want more _____.

I want less _____.

● ● ●

D o you have anything left to give?

Helping while you're depleted is a breeding ground for resentment and burnout.

Prioritize being a healthy helper.

Prioritize being well and doing good for others.

Nurturing yourself is an integral part of being capable of nurturing others.

CONSIDER THIS:

While caring for others, I can take care of myself in the following ways . . .

● ● ●

We live in an age of information at our fingertips. Social media snippets of information are given to break down complicated topics. As a result, we should assume that some things have been left unsaid.

For instance, "You contribute to your problems" is a blanket statement that doesn't apply to all situations. You weren't the cause of someone abusing you or hitting your car. Conversely, in a relationship where you withheld emotions and the other person pulled away, there was a cause and effect. Complicated scenarios cannot be explained in simple lines of thought.

Social media provides widespread information on a variety of topics, but it's important to consider the source and meaning. Read and think critically.

● ● ●

Rewire your thinking about guilt.

I often wonder if we use the word "guilt" as a cover for other emotions like

▸ *Sadness*

▸ *Disappointment in ourselves*

▸ *The perception that we've disappointed someone else*

▸ *Longing*

You can experience guilt when you're making a healthy and wise decision.

Guilt doesn't mean you're doing a bad thing. It can also mean you're operating in an uncomfortable space.

Sometimes, when I am experiencing "mom guilt" about time spent away from my kids, I am actually just missing my kids. Guilt can be a reaction to doing something wrong or simply *feeling as though* you're doing something wrong. It's not inherently wrong to be away from my kids, so there isn't anything for me to feel guilty about.

When we feel guilty, we need to see what is really at the core of it. To uncover if you're actually feeling guilty, ask yourself:

▸ *Am I doing something wrong?*

▸ *Have other people identified what I've done as bad? If so, why?*

▸ *If others have identified it as bad, why is it bad?*

▸ *Is what I've done against the law, or socially unacceptable?*

▸ *Is what I've done socially unacceptable?*

▸ *Does what I've done hurt someone else in a meaningful way?*

● ● ●

I went on a road trip with someone who was in charge of reading the directions as I drove. During this time, there was no GPS in cars, so we printed directions before we left home. Somehow, we missed a turn, and we drove out of the way. I asked, "Are we lost?"

My co-roadtripper said, "No, you're going the right way."

After about thirty minutes, I declared, "We're lost." I grabbed the directions, and sure enough, I could tell we'd missed a pivotal turn.

My co-roadtripper immediately said, "It wasn't my fault. I didn't see it."

Pointing the finger doesn't require effort. It's no surprise that many of us struggle with being held accountable. We don't want to view ourselves as having made a mistake or as a bad person.

But making a bad choice, saying the wrong thing, or mistreating someone doesn't make you a bad person.

However, if you think you can never do wrong in your relationships, that's problematic. It can be hard to maintain a relationship with a person who is supposedly *never* at fault.

There is always time to self-correct and choose to do better. Not acknowledging your faults will cause problems in your relationships.

● ● ●

It's easy if you try.

—John Lennon, "Imagine"

I t isn't easy." Sometimes, we say this to convince ourselves that what we want isn't worth the effort or won't work.

But easy things are not the only worthy pursuits.

Affirmations:

▸ *Life requires effort.*

▸ *Hard things have been done.*

▸ *I might surprise myself.*

Challenge yourself to be amazed by what you can do when you try.

Challenge yourself to try a different approach to something that wasn't easy the first time.

But don't let "it isn't easy" stop you from doing things that might transform, inspire, or heal you.

● ● ●

W hen you stop chasing perfection, you'll become content with enough.

Perfection is impossible, but we seek it as a way to be our best, be seen as the best, and keep ourselves occupied. Allowing things to be enough gives you the freedom to be content without the need to constantly strive for better.

Contentment doesn't end ambition, but it allows you to be enough.

● ● ●

H ave a good cry. It's cathartic.

Tears have meaning and reveal more than just sadness.
Sometimes, you cry because you're struggling to be
heard, you don't feel seen, or you're overwhelmed, excited,
or afraid.

A few days a month, I notice I am more easily prone to tears
than on other days. Have you noticed that you are more likely
to cry at a particular time of month, during a certain season, or
when faced with a specific trigger?

Some people don't cry because it seems like a weakness.
They might want to cry but have been holding it in so long
that they find it hard to release tears.

Tears cannot be forced, but they also shouldn't be withheld.
Allow tears to flow naturally. Letting it out is therapeutic.

● ● ●

S ometimes, the unhappiness comes from inside you. It isn't coming from anything around you.

When you're displeased, unclear, or in despair, it will seem like that feeling has been caused by other people. It will seem like changing something outside yourself will make things better.

Signs that it's coming from inside include:

▸ *You feel the same way no matter who you're around.*

▸ *You have moved locations and yet feel the same.*

▸ *There's a pattern of mood lows.*

▸ *The other person didn't do anything harmful or unreasonable.*

▸ *Everyone annoys you, not just a few.*

Blaming others for internal struggles will keep you unhealed. When you acknowledge "It was me all along," you can move toward working on the parts of yourself that need healing.

Lean inward.

● ● ●

One of the hardest things about grief is the expectation that you should return to normal after a short time.

Grief is not time-limited; it's an emotional experience that lasts for an undefined period of time. Grieving happens moment to moment. You might feel fine one minute and start sobbing the next. Prolonged grief is a normal response to love. Feel what you feel for as long as you need.

The residual effect of losing someone or something is that people around you will move on while you grieve. People will fail to consider that you are still grieving.

Grief is individual even when you are in community with others. People experience it differently even when the loss is similar.

●　●　●

S omeone told me about a short-tempered flight attendant that she'd encountered. She chose to remain calm and pleasant, and at the end of the flight, the flight attendant thanked her for it.

When people are stressed or going through something, it might have an impact on how they treat others.

When a stranger seems moody, a coworker's attitude isn't what you expect, or your friend is being overly direct, they might not be okay. Remember that it isn't personal.

● ● ●

Willpower is not an option for everyone.

"Just be happy" isn't so simple.

Choose your words wisely.

Simple words cannot tackle complicated problems. Although you may mean well, the issue might be deeper than meets the eye.

● ● ●

N otice yourself over-applying new ideas.

It has become common practice to throw around clinical terms in a casual way. When we're particular about how we organize our home, we say we're "OCD," when we're actually just organized. When someone ignores us or is inconsiderate of our feelings, we call them a "narcissist." We turn them into a bad person, when the truth is likely much more complex.

OCD is not about being organized. Obsessive-compulsive disorder is when you have compulsive thoughts or behaviors that are seen as unreasonable. For example, when you have OCD, you don't organize; you feel anxious or depressed. You have some sort of repetitive behavior that you must do. It goes far beyond a desire to keep a clean home.

When we come across new information, we tend to view it from a simplistic lens.

Be mindful when applying a term.

● ● ●

Sustainable relationships require maintenance. When we don't know how to take care of our relationships, we usually give up and pursue a new one. But the problem will recur because we lack an essential skill.

Maintain what already exists before venturing out to acquire more. Someone asked, "How many friends should I have?" There's no set amount. A healthy number of relationships is the amount you can maintain. Some of us are overflowing with connections that we struggle to sustain.

The skills you use to acquire relationships are similar to what you need to maintain them: openness, respect, willingness, kindness, and time.

● ● ●

G rieve for the younger version of yourself that didn't know any better, needed protection, or did what was required to survive. Don't be ashamed of what you had to do.

Shame is bondage.

Affirmations:

▸ *Adapting to my environment made sense at the time.*

▸ *I did what I could with the tools I had.*

▸ *I survived by using the skills I had.*

Honesty and acceptance are the path to peace.

I hope you learn to live with all of yourself.

● ● ●

When dealing with our closest loved ones, we don't always give them our best. One of the reasons for that is that our self-sabotage can kick into overdrive. We sometimes test the love and connection we are being offered. We can do and say all kinds of hurtful things to push the people we care about to their limit, and then when they leave, we say, "I was right all along—I knew they would leave." Sometimes we're not even conscious of this behavior, and being unaware of our pattern leads us to repeat it.

Some of the other reasons we don't show up as our best selves with people we care about are:

- *We think that because people care about us, they will tolerate anything we throw at them.*

- *We think that the trust we have with others entitles us to hand them all of our difficult stuff, expecting them to hold it for us.*

- *We are unaware of what we're doing and don't realize the impact it is having.*

● ● ●

D o one thing at a time.

Examples:

▸ *Drive in silence.*

▸ *Read a book, and leave your phone in another room.*

▸ *Listen intently.*

▸ *Watch television without also scrolling on your phone.*

Whenever I attempt to write notes for work while watching television, it takes me much longer to complete them. There are so many tasks that I have grown accustomed to bundling with other ones.

We now live in an age where it takes skill and practice to focus on one thing. Pull your focus toward one important thing instead of multiple things at once.

• • •

Trust is built through honesty and accountability.

When people learn that they can't trust what you say or that you refuse to be accountable, the disappointment pushes them away (either emotionally or physically).

Honesty is a show of integrity and a willingness to be seen as imperfect.

Even in the small things, operate with integrity.

I hope you say these phrases often:

It was my fault.

I made a mistake.

To be honest . . .

• • •

When you feel triggered, it's an indication that you have feelings that need to be felt or inner work you need to do.

Two things that help:

▸ *Making room to feel*

▸ *Wondering what your feelings might mean*

Things that don't help:

▸ *Verbally minimizing your triggers*

▸ *Exposing yourself to triggers without addressing the underlying feelings*

▸ *Ignoring triggers*

● ● ●

Your energy, attitude, and conversation style shift when you're in the company of certain people.

When you find yourself withholding, or being short, agitated, or angry, listen to what your feelings are telling you. The discomfort is your gut reaction.

Feelings offer information.

CONSIDER THIS:

Do you need to have a conversation about an issue with the other person?

Do you need to change your perspective about an issue?

Would it be beneficial to explore new boundaries in the relationship?

Could some distance help the situation?

What would you like to do next time?

Are you silently dealing with things you need to address?

Sit with your feelings, and determine how you want to act. Don't let anger or hurt fester.

● ● ●

Choose quality over quantity.

Deep relationships sustain you.

Relationships that lack depth may leave you feeling
that something is missing. More relationships won't provide
deeper connections.

Three deep relationships feel like plenty when they are
authentic, caring, and honoring.

Twenty relationships that lack depth will feel empty.

It's the substance of the relationships that matters, and substance
requires that we be vulnerable with others.

Ask Yourself:

▸ *How many relationships are you deeply invested in?*

▸ *How can you create more vulnerable relationships?*

● ● ●

S tate what you mean simply.

When my youngest daughter was two years old, she said, "I don't like it." This phrase was used to advocate for what she wore and what she ate. It was simple, so I easily understood her meaning.

Adults use a lot of words to say simple things. For example, an adult might cancel plans using the following statements, "My mother is coming into town. My house isn't clean, so I have to go to the grocery store before picking her up from the airport. I really want to be at your dinner, but I don't think I can make it with everything I have going on. Can you please forgive me? I should have planned this better." A simple way to say the same thing might be, "I didn't plan my time well. I can't make it to dinner."

Add these simple phrases to your repertoire:

▸ *"I don't like it."*

▸ *"I made a mistake."*

▸ *"I don't feel good about this."*

▸ *"I don't want that anymore."*

These statements are enough.

Believe the other person can manage their emotions. When you overexplain, CONSIDER THIS:

Are you assuming the worst?

Is the person truly incapable of managing their reaction?

Is it your job to manage their reaction?

● ● ●

When you truly look at yourself, you will find that you won't have time to focus on other people's business. Your life will keep you busy enough.

Being overly involved in the lives of others can be a sign that you are neglecting or avoiding your own life. You have so many things that require your attention.

When you feel the desire to wander into someone else's business, make sure you've done the following:

▸ *Had enough water during the day*

▸ *Watered your grass, garden, and/or plants*

▸ *Spent time journaling*

▸ *Made a list of your goals*

▸ *Taken care of your household*

▸ *Managed your life*

When you find yourself focused on others, look within.

● ● ●

Choose what you're willing to give up now for a greater outcome later. Sacrifices are needed to get where you want to go.

This is the part that isn't easy. People who desire to become Olympic athletes often spend months or years away from their families to train for their goal.

▸ *What are you willing to release to have what you truly want?*

▸ *What are you willing to do less of to have something else you desire?*

We often attribute our inability to accomplish something to a lack of time when it's really a lack of willingness to sacrifice.

You can't have it all at the same time. When we see the highlights of someone's life on social media, we don't usually see the sacrifices they've made to produce their photos and videos.

Prioritize, prioritize, prioritize . . . and make sacrifices where needed.

● ● ●

When you read a text that seems hostile, try rereading it with a big smile. We can assume tone without knowing the context. Sometimes, a text is just a text and not what we think it means.

When you communicate via text, email, or even phone, it can be hard to discern what the other person is feeling. When you sense attitude, shortness, or a cold response, pause and think about the story you're creating. Consider if it's appropriate to address the mood or tone. Maybe you have misunderstood.

Notice the stories you tell yourself. What context are you adding that might not be there?

● ● ●

A friend of mine recently found out that someone she knows on social media is getting a divorce. She went through several posts, trying to find out about the breakup. All she found were seemingly happy pictures of the couple, celebrating and cheering each other on.

What's more important to you—what people see or what is true?

The inside is where you dwell. The way you are with your partner privately is what matters in your relationship. The internal and external can align, but if everything is external, you will feel emotionally dissatisfied.

While you don't have to disclose everything about yourself to the outside world, does what you present externally match your internal self, or is it false?

● ● ●

Sometimes, it's a peaceful decision to end relationships with certain people.

You might feel both relief and guilt, because we've been taught to feel bad about ourselves when we make choices that are healthy for us but perhaps hurtful for the other person. If you stay because you feel too bad to leave, you will still feel guilt. You'll have "I don't want this relationship" guilt.

Your behavior will reflect your mental state, which could look like

▸ *Isolating the other person emotionally*

▸ *Avoiding time with them*

▸ *Feelings of anxiety in their presence*

▸ *Bouts of sadness or depression before or after interacting with them*

This is nothing to feel bad about.

● ● ●

We have surface-level relationships with people we see and speak to often. Frequent contact with a coworker isn't indicative of a deeper connection. Speaking to someone often isn't a measure of closeness. Depth determines closeness.

What you talk about is more important than how often you speak to someone.

Go deeper if you want to feel more connected.

• • •

W e can lead people to accountability by normalizing mistakes instead of shaming people for them. Shame doesn't change behavior; it only makes us become secretive.

Everyone makes mistakes, and the grace you want when you make one is the same grace you can offer to others.

Before harshly criticizing someone, remember your own mistakes, and remember what you needed to hear.

Here are a few mistakes I made recently:

▸ *Set my cup of drinking water too close to my oil diffuser. It was quite gross when I took a sip.*

▸ *Left a piece of chocolate in my pocket. Side note: I really need to learn from this. It has happened to me too many times.*

▸ *Told someone what they should do instead of letting them figure out their own problem.*

Take note:

▸ *I recently made the following mistakes . . .*

Be kind, and remember that mistakes are part of everyone's learning process.

● ● ●

Time can't be rushed.

Patience is the only choice, even when you don't like it. People lament, "I need to be patient." But you actually have no choice. You will either wait calmly, or you will wait in a mood. Either way, you will wait. Perhaps, what you need is to feel calmer or less moody.

Sometimes, this means allowing for extra time when you plan.

Traffic will take time.

Waiting on others will take time.

Progress on a goal will take time.

Who you become while waiting matters. Do you complain? Do you pace? Do you check the time repeatedly? Do you try to speed things up secretly, knowing you can't? How do you handle something you can't control?

You will have to wait on some things. Your job is determining who you will be while practicing patience.

● ● ●

Gabriel wanted his father to take more interest in his life. He wanted to hear "I'm proud of you" when he purchased a house. With each new interaction with his dad, Gabriel's longing for approval made him more sad. It was hard for him to accept his father as he was.

When someone doesn't fulfill your expectations or desires, you may long for what isn't possible with them. It's a kind of grief.

Even if/when you decide to end the relationship, the longing might not leave.

Some situations simply don't have a happy ending. But acceptance is possible and can bring you peace.

● ● ●

It can be uncomfortable when our desires for a relationship don't match up with someone else's. This doesn't always require a conversation, but it does require recognition. We have to make peace with the fact that what we desire is only as important as the other person desiring it. We can't demand that a person call us once a week if they are not interested in communicating with us that often. We have to look at people's behaviors, and their interactions with us, and receive the information they are offering.

Is this person not

▸ *Answering your calls?*

▸ *Responding to your text messages?*

▸ *Inviting you to social events?*

▸ *Confiding in you?*

If this is happening, this person is telling us something. They are not making themselves available to us for a reason. Now, there are times when we are in a close relationship and these things are happening, in which case a conversation is necessary. There are other times when people are just not as interested in us as we are in them.

● ● ●

Your problems aren't more significant than anyone else's.

It's never helpful to say you have a bigger problem than someone else or to diminish someone else's feelings about their problems.

Problems are unique to the individuals who experience them, and our responses to similar circumstances might be different. For instance, my fifteen-year-old client was distracted by her breakup while her parents opined, "She'll get over it." It wasn't helpful for her to hear that from them, even if they felt it was true.

We all go through difficulties in our own way and to our own level of understanding and maturity.

Things you can handle may be challenging to others.

Things someone else has powered through might break you down.

CONSIDER THIS:

When have you found it hard to have empathy for others?

What feels comforting to hear when you're going through something?

What do you wish others wouldn't say when you're going through something?

● ● ●

B etraying your "nevers" is a part of growth.

Rather than say something like "I would never . . . ," we should think about changing our language to "I don't *think* I would ever . . ." or "I'm not yet in a place where I would . . ." We can express preferences without excluding other options. Most of us have not lived enough to commit to "never."

Maturity teaches us that we don't need to use the term "never" often because we change our minds again and again. We don't have to stick to being the person we were in fourth grade or even last year. We don't have to resist something we want to try because of our commitment to never changing.

We generate a lot of shame when we don't allow ourselves to change. We're not only stuck on "Who am I?" but we're also afraid to tell anyone else who we are. Flexibility about who we are allows us to be more true to ourselves and to be more open and honest with others.

● ● ●

We can become so focused on other people's lives that we miss out on opportunities for reflection and introspection. Sometimes, our fixation on other people's stories can make us forget what stories belong to us.

Moving further away from yourself can look like being overly involved in the lives, doings, and business of others.

CONSIDER THIS:

What would life be like if you spent more time learning about yourself?

What would your relationships be like if you were clearer about your values?

● ● ●

A voiding human discomfort increases human discomfort.

The more we move away from problems, the more problematic they become.

Procrastination is avoidance. And we know that the more we procrastinate, the more pressure we feel to meet the deadline.

Avoiding hard conversations makes us feel resentful, stressed, and isolated.

Discomfort can be an invitation to

▸ *Approach your life differently*

▸ *Figure out how to change the way you exist inside a relationship*

▸ *Shift a role you have taken on in your life*

▸ *Change your environment*

Avoidance is not a comfort; it's a distraction.

● ● ●

When you don't show up, people will stop asking you to show up.

When you frequently decline invitations, people will ask you less often.

When you exhibit poor listening skills, people will stop sharing with you.

People react behaviorally based on what they receive or don't receive from you.

Life doesn't happen without cause and effect. Notice what happens before and after.

● ● ●

E veryone's feedback is not valuable, and you decide who to listen to.

Some people are biased.

Some people attempt to get you to do what they haven't tried.

Some people aren't a good resource.

Try to discern when it's appropriate to offer advice. In some relationships, we give and receive advice freely, but that isn't true of every relationship. When you're the one giving advice, take the time to think about whether it's truly of value. Avoid imposing on someone else what you would do.

When someone is interested in receiving advice from you, they will

- *Tell you they appreciate it*

- *Ask you for advice on a number of occasions*

- *Share how they applied the advice you gave them*

On the other hand, these behaviors would indicate that someone is not interested in or receptive to your advice:

- *There is no engagement when you offer advice. Instead, you are met with silence.*

- *They don't apply your guidance.*

● ● ●

M ental and physical health go hand in hand. Taking care of your mental health is synonymous with caring for your physical health. Stress impacts your body, and prolonged stress contributes to severe health conditions.

It's helpful to note how stress can manifest in your body:

▶ *Do you get headaches or migraines?*

▶ *Are you constantly sick?*

▶ *Do you develop skin rashes?*

▶ *Does your eye twitch?*

▶ *Do you have stomach issues?*

You already have an idea of what causes you stress. Can you enter those situations differently? Is it possible that some situations must stop or pause?

Remember that you have one body, and it's connected to your mind and spirit. When you make decisions, stay mindful of your mental and physical health.

● ● ●

Rules can be helpful, but sometimes we create rules that box us in. Make sure your rules are not a prison. It's healthy to be flexible about the rules you create for yourself.

Rules can be healthy when they keep you safe and allow you to live well, but they are damaging when they keep you stuck, frustrated, or anxious.

CONSIDER THIS:

Who are your rules meant to protect?

What values do your rules uphold?

Do they harm others?

Are they harming you?

Rules can either trap you or enhance your life.

▸ *What self-imposed rules are you willing to break to live more fully?*

● ● ●

I magine yourself at a gathering, filling a paper plate with food. Someone asks you to add more food for them. Then, another person asks you to add some food for them as well. Eventually, you run out of space, your plate crumbles under the weight, and you kindly let them know "my plate is already full."

You *cannot* do it all. You will need help from others to operate at your most remarkable capacity.

When you agree to do more, remove something else from your plate. As you add more roles, determine what else needs to shift.

Writing projects require me to reduce my time on social media, hold off on meetings, and decrease my caseload. While it's possible to do all these things at once, it would certainly leave me feeling exhausted.

Time is what it has always been. It's just twenty-four hours per day. Unlearn spreading yourself thin, and start subtracting as you add more.

● ● ●

Poor communication is one of the top three reasons for divorce.

I started counseling Trent and Michael when they were on the brink of a breakup. Whenever they communicated, they argued. Neither ever felt understood or heard. At first, they got along well and argued very little. Once the honeymoon phase was over, they found that a way of avoiding conflict was by not speaking to each other.

There's a tendency in relationships to let issues go because we don't want to seem petty. But under-communication is more problematic than over-communication. Not talking about an issue usually allows resentment and frustration to build—not to go away.

Your friends, family members, coworkers, therapist, etc., shouldn't be the only people to know your issues in your primary relationship. Speak directly to your partner about what's on your mind. Don't avoid communicating because you don't want to be challenged. Learn how to communicate better, and encourage your partner to do the same.

● ● ●

N uance moment: Should you take the high road or address the issue?

There's a fine line between letting it go and not standing up for yourself.

CONSIDER THIS when you're trying to determine what to do:

What are the presumed intentions of the other person?

Is this a routine issue with the same person?

Is it safe to respond?

Can you tolerate how they might react?

Will remaining silent impact others?

● ● ●

After having my first daughter, I returned to the gym. While lying down, I could not lift my feet off the ground to perform an abdominal exercise. I immediately thought I would never be able to do the exercise again, so I moved on to other exercises that I could perform. Each workout, I painfully revisited the same exercise, each time with slight improvement. Eventually, I rejoiced when I was able to hold both of my feet in the air for an isometric contraction.

Discipline is the commitment to reaching a goal, sometimes without enjoying the process.

There will be aspects that you love and aspects you dislike on the path to achieving a goal. When some of us reach a point of discomfort, we quit, while others keep going. Or you may find yourself disciplined while working toward one goal but not while working toward another.

Discipline is a practice. Many of us need more practice moving through the entire process, not just the parts we enjoy.

CONSIDER THIS:

What discipline practices do you do well?

What barriers tend to get in the way of your commitment and discipline?

• • •

Making a choice without putting pressure on yourself to get it right looks like:

- Asking yourself why it matters. *If you feel that you must make the perfect decision, remind yourself that perfection doesn't exist. Lean into your preference and what feels good to you.*

- Giving yourself the opportunity to fail. *It's okay if the choice you make doesn't go the way you thought it would. It's okay to start over and choose something else.*

- Allowing yourself to try something new. *Take a chance, and step outside of your comfort zone.*

- Being honest with yourself about the consequences. *What is the worst that could happen if you choose one option over another? Are there any consequences at all?*

Sometimes, there is no right decision, just the decision you make.

● ● ●

For many years, you may have believed that you can only rest and play after your chores and duties are done.

You're an adult now, so you can rest while dishes are in the sink. You can go out with friends even if the laundry isn't done.

Being an adult comes with many responsibilities, and it's an unreasonable expectation to stay on top of everything all the time. You deserve to rest and play. If you wait until everything is complete, you will live a rigid and unfulfilling life.

It can be appropriate at times to put a task aside for a little while.

CONSIDER THIS:

What's something you can set aside to engage in a joyful or pleasurable activity?

• • •

Amy was concerned about her father's health because he was getting older and lived on his own. She was the only one of her siblings without children and deeply into her career. She believed her only option was to allow her father to move in with her and cut back on work.

I explored the possibilities with her, such as soliciting help from others while her father remained in his own space.

You can decide how you want to show up in your relationships (all types of relationships).

Sometimes, you are doing too much without appreciation.

Sometimes, your boundaries need to be respected.

You don't "have to" do what's expected of you. Get creative.

CONSIDER THIS:

How can you approach your situation differently?

Are you over-giving? If so, should you pull back?

You are not disempowered. Perhaps you feel that way because the other person is deciding for you, but you have the power to choose for yourself.

● ● ●

We all reach conclusions in our own time.

Others can't speed us up, and we can't speed someone else up. We each arrive on our own timeline.

Repeat After Me:

I cannot determine someone else's timing.

It's painful and exhausting to watch as someone makes a mess of their life, but what you can control is whether or not you watch.

If someone wants to tell you about their relationship challenges, for example, you can choose to discuss other topics with them.

We can't push people in other directions when we're tired of seeing them suffer. They have to be ready, and they have to want what we see for them.

Sadly, some people are not ready.

• • •

We don't always get what we want, but that has nothing to do with being deserving.

Life happens, and we can't control the way it unfolds. There's a general belief that if we work hard enough, we'll eventually get what we most want. But this isn't always the case, and it's no reflection of our efforts. Some things are simply not meant to work out.

Perhaps, instead of avoiding pain, we must learn to manage it when it appears.

How do you tend to your feelings of disappointment when something doesn't go your way?

Be gentle with yourself as you recover from not getting what you want.

● ● ●

The healthiest way to manage feelings is to feel them.

People come to therapy with the intention of learning how to feel less. "I'm anxious. How do I stop it?" But I help people discover what's behind the feelings and how to sit with the discomfort. Eventually, even though their feelings are still present, they notice that the emotions are less intense.

You become more deeply connected with yourself as you feel.

You become more connected with others as you feel.

Emotions are hard in a culture that has encouraged us to push them aside. Reclaim what you feel.

● ● ●

On weekends, Veronica often found it hard to relax. She kept herself busy. When the pandemic arrived, she was lost without her typical outlets for busyness. Gradually, since she couldn't control her level of busyness anymore, she learned to embrace doing nothing.

When inaction makes you uncomfortable, wonder why you feel more comfortable doing than just being. Develop a practice of sitting with yourself to check in, restore, and reflect. Process what happens when you allow yourself to be still.

The discomfort with being still is often simply due to a lack of practice.

● ● ●

Perhaps this is the day, month, or year you become more of yourself.

May you set healthier boundaries.

May you become more aware of your strengths.

May you make decisions aligned with your goals.

May you connect on a deeper level with the people you love.

The difference between yesterday and today is you.

You are the deciding factor.

There's no magical time to make changes. So don't hold off until the beginning of the year to do something you've been considering today. Set goals, and honor them passionately.

● ● ●

Everything may not be aligned at the same time.

Work can be going well while your romantic relationship isn't. Parenting can be going well while work is not.

Adulthood is learning the skill of doing multiple things simultaneously and understanding that everything may not be great at the same time. We try to balance it all, but perhaps we need to accept that everything will have its time and place.

Your life may not be aligned in every area at the same time, but you can still appreciate the good things when you have them.

● ● ●

L ife is unpredictable. Therefore, we can't have a plan for everything.

It's sometimes helpful to consider what's likely to happen, but life is full of surprises and unplanned moments.

Constant perfection is impossible in a world full of factors you can't control.

Be more flexible in your planning, thinking, and expectations.

Peacefully accept that not everything will go according to plan.

● ● ●

I t requires trust to allow people to help you when you've become accustomed to doing everything yourself.

Here are a few ways to keep yourself from falling into the trap of doing everything alone:

- *Determine whether you are doing something by yourself because **(1)** you want the glory of saying you did it, **(2)** you don't have anyone else to help you, or **(3)** you're good at it and enjoy it.*

- *Ask for help. Allow yourself to be supported and give others the chance to support you.*

- *Express gratitude. Acknowledge how the efforts and achievements of others contribute to what you accomplish.*

Affirmations:

▸ *I trust that people can care for me.*

▸ *I trust that their care for me is rooted in love.*

▸ *I trust that I'm in good hands.*

▸ *I trust that someone else will handle the situation when I release control.*

▸ *I trust that others are capable.*

▸ *I can care for myself and understand the power of not doing things alone.*

● ● ●

A friend has a candy bowl in her office. Some people take one or two pieces, and others grab by the handful.

When you give people open access to you, they may take more than you have to offer or more than you would like.

Setting limits keeps you from feeling depleted.

• • •

If you struggle to apologize for something you did, examine why.

Things that keep us from apologizing:

- **We don't want to be seen as wrong.** *We worry that saying we're sorry will make us look weird or stupid. We worry that apologizing is admitting to a poor choice, which will reflect poorly on our overall character.*

- **Our ego gets in the way.** *We have a hard time owning mistakes. We are more concerned with being right than with preserving and caring for our relationships.*

- **We have difficulty recognizing our impact.** *We can be blind to the ways in which our words and actions affect people. It's a kind of protective denial that shields us from the harm we cause.*

Accountability builds character. Insincere apologies placate but don't repair relationships.

● ● ●

D errick very kindly told his best friend that he couldn't loan him $5,000. He didn't want to loan such a large amount to his friend, who had a track record of not paying him back. As a result, his friend stopped answering Derrick's calls and texts. After setting a boundary, Derrick lost his best friend.

A side effect of growth is losing people who liked you better when you were without boundaries or engaged in behaviors similar to their own.

Relationships end, but that doesn't mean you're a failure.

Sometimes, people aren't in our lives forever because they aren't meant to be. Hopefully, we learn about ourselves from each person who touches our lives, no matter the length of their presence.

Boundaries are needed even when there is a possibility that the relationship will change.

● ● ●

The special occasion may not come. Use the good stuff, or wear the nice outfit now.

Every day is special, and things are meant to be used, not collected (unless collecting is your goal). Far too many of us miss the opportunity to use what we worked hard to acquire, waiting for some illusive big moment. Use your beautiful things now.

• • •

Your problems are a big deal to you, and other people's problems are a big deal to them. There is no Olympic medal for the biggest sufferer, so stop competing.

A six-year-old's biggest problem might be that a friend doesn't want to play with them.

An eighteen-year-old's biggest problem might be figuring out college life and being away from home.

A forty-year-old's biggest problem might be a pending separation from a partner.

All the above problems matter and feel intense to the people experiencing them. There's no hierarchy of suffering, because so much is based on who we are and what has happened to us in the past.

• • •

P assive-aggressive behavior comes from anger and frustration. It can be triggered by sadness or hurt, or when we feel someone has taken advantage of us. Many of us behave in a passive-aggressive manner because we believe we can't be honest about what we feel.

You can prevent yourself from being passive-aggressive by speaking up.

Here are some tips:

- *Try not to use words like "always" or "every time." Just focus on that moment. You can say "I was trying to say something, and you cut me off. Can I finish?" Or "It sounds like you're trying to be helpful, but you're telling me what to do. I need to listen to myself in this situation."*

- *Even if you don't know exactly how to explain what you're feeling, you can say "Oh, I didn't like that" or "Something about that made me feel off."*

- *Remember that when you speak up, you won't feel like you betrayed yourself by keeping quiet.*

- *Recognize that folks may not realize they've offended you unless you tell them. We all have different humor and pain points. They may need you to say "Jokes like that aren't funny to me."*

- *Be honest about what works for you. Speak your truth even if the person receiving it may not understand it. If, for example, they insist that everyone else loves their jokes, it's okay that you don't, as long as they respect that. Let them know that it just isn't your brand of humor.*

- *Take preventative measures where appropriate. If you know you are going to have an interaction with someone who might trigger your frustration, warn them beforehand. For instance, if you're going to the library with a friend who is always loud and that bothers you, say "Hey, we're about to go into the library, remember to keep your voice down." Prevent your irritation when you can.*

● ● ●

I t's hard to own the parts of ourselves that don't excel, because in our society, we tend to highlight only where our talents lie. Just look at social media. Many people's pages are a highlight reel.

Sometimes, we feel bad when we aren't great at something, but no one can be great at everything. We want to be top tier, and when we can't, we feel it's a problem we have to fix. But that's part of being human. We are imperfect.

● ● ●

C onfirmation bias is looking for and listening to information that supports what you want to see or hear. It feels wonderful to be validated, but it's limiting when we ignore other points of view.

Even when we don't want to apply other facts, it's helpful to at least acknowledge that other truths exist.

Your perspective is rarely the only one.

● ● ●

Y ou are half of any relationship you're in.

We assume the easy path to improving a relationship is getting the other person to change. Do you think "If they would just _____, then _____ would be okay"?

Unless the relationship is abusive, it's rare that all of the issues belong to one person. Taking responsibility for your part in your relationship's problems will help to resolve them.

● ● ●

There is a misconception that if we have negative thoughts, the best way to combat them is to turn them off and turn on happy, positive thoughts. We think that drowning out our negative thoughts will make us feel better, but this completely skips over the truth of what we're feeling.

It's okay to talk ourselves through challenging situations with positive statements, but we can do that while still acknowledging that we're upset. Positive thinking is great when it's authentic, but when we force it while feeling sad, disappointed, frustrated, or angry, it prolongs these uncomfortable emotions. We don't need to drown out how we're feeling with faux positivity.

● ● ●

The content of your words, not necessarily the amount of words delivered, makes you a skillful communicator. It's possible to say a lot without getting to the point.

Saying more can confuse the listener.

Saying more can cause people to get off topic.

Saying more can cause people to miss your point.

Less is often more when communicating a need, delivering a complex message, or working through a challenge. Clear communication can be concise and brief.

Say what you need to say to get to the heart of your message, but don't say more than necessary.

● ● ●

L ove requires action, not simply words.

"I love you" should be followed by many loving acts.

▸ *Kindness is love.*

▸ *Respect is love.*

▸ *Gentleness is love.*

▸ *Safety is love.*

▸ *Mistreatment is not love.*

▸ *Meanness is not love.*

▸ *Shaming is not love.*

▸ *Abuse is not love.*

Loving someone isn't a commitment to tolerating anything from them. They have to love and care for you in return.

● ● ●

I ndependence is freedom, but it doesn't mean you operate alone. Learn to receive support from others gracefully.

When people offer, accept.

Tell them when they ask "What do you need?"

Burnout and depletion are not noble. Staying healthy both emotionally and physically requires some level of support from others.

● ● ●

C larity takes time, so you don't have to figure everything out right away.

In the meantime, let your mind rest while you're in limbo.

Forcing yourself to figure something out may be a sign that you aren't ready for what's next. Perhaps your work is figuring out how to exist without certainty.

● ● ●

People may not understand what you're going through when they have limited experience with your struggle.

People may not understand what you're going through when they have handled similar experiences differently.

People may not understand what you're going through when their own experiences consume them.

This doesn't mean that you are alone. You simply haven't yet found people who can relate to you.

●　●　●

You will regret shrinking yourself to accommodate the insecurities of others. Surely, you will resent the other person when you give up parts of yourself to accommodate the relationship.

Guard against compromising what's most important to you just for the sake of getting along.

CONSIDER THIS:

What parts of you have you hidden in relationships?

Have confidence that there exist people who possess the capacity to be present with you in your authentic state.

● ● ●

Not everything you start must be finished. Some activities are worth just a short-term exploration.

You don't have to pressure yourself to commit to everything you try.

Doing something new for two weeks may be enough time to know it isn't for you.

Not everything or everyone is right for you, and not everything is meant to last.

● ● ●

W e set ourselves up for disappointment when we create expectations that are assigned to certain ages.

If you find yourself getting stuck in this line of thinking, you can reframe your aspirations by

- **Setting reasonable goals.** *Set goals based on where you are in life, because if it's not reasonable, it's a wish, not a goal.*

- **Starting with a couple of (reasonable) goals.** *Rome wasn't built in a day. You don't have to tackle everything at the same time.*

- **Giving yourself grace when you don't meet your goals.** *Life happens and things don't always go according to plan.*

- **Removing age limitations from your goals.** *Don't use the number, just have your goal.*

We can all defy expectations of our age. We don't have to do anything by the age of _____ unless we want to and have a lifestyle that supports us being able to do that.

● ● ●

It isn't possible to like everyone, and that's okay.

But you can dislike people without being mean to them.

Say "good morning" to the coworker who sends
rude emails.

Offer a smile to the neighbor who doesn't speak to you.

It takes more energy to go out of your way to be mean than
it does to be cordial.

You have to exist in a world with people you don't like.
Make the experiences less draining when you can.

● ● ●

S elf-care involves wondering what you need right now to feel restored and well.

Self-care can mean many different things based on your individual needs. Perhaps it's calling a friend for a brief chat, sleeping in, waking up early before everyone else to enjoy some quiet time, or pushing yourself to get out because you know you'll have fun connecting with others.

Self-care is not universal. What feels nurturing to you may not feel nurturing to others. Often, it's necessary for me to wake up early to grab some peace, but you might need to sleep in to feel restored. I have to tune in to myself in the moment, because sometimes sleeping in is also what I need.

Your needs are flexible, so your self-care practices must be as well.

CONSIDER THIS:

What do you need, and how can you pursue it?

● ● ●

It's an ongoing practice to find balance between not caring, caring too much, and caring what the wrong people think.

Sometimes, you can't care what others think and still be honest.

Sometimes, you can't care what others think and still be good.

Sometimes, you can't care what others think, because it will ruin your relationships.

Sometimes, you can't care what others think, because it will derail your focus.

Caring about what others think may not be consistent with your integrity.

Believe that you can manage the discomfort of not having everyone's approval.

● ● ●

Wild ideas can turn into flourishing businesses.

Dreams sound impossible to those who don't understand them.

Most of the things we can't live without and the products we consume were once wild ideas.

Be careful not to place limits on what's possible. Develop a new mentality called "find a way."

Limited thinking disables dreams.

● ● ●

I love getting the newest version of the iPhone. It's like Christmas for me whenever it comes out. But if you have a smartphone, you know it's constantly updating. Every time you turn around, you're being asked to install the latest version of the software. And when you install that software, it takes a little while for the phone to run smoothly.

The creators may have to run through a few versions of each update before they work out glitches. The phone doesn't have to be perfect, and we don't have to be either.

Being perfect is an unattainable goal because

- *Perfection is rooted in our need to please other people, but it's impossible to please everyone. When someone doesn't like you, it doesn't mean anything is wrong with you. It's just about their preference.*

- *Most things need to be updated. We are constant works in progress, just like our phones. We apply lessons as we learn and grow.*

- *We can't control everything.*

- *We are human beings, which inherently means that we are imperfect.*

● ● ●

You will resent giving to others if it means you are neglecting yourself.

Helping when you are well is a contribution.

Helping when you are unwell is a burden.

Take care of yourself first and then others.

● ● ●

C hanging your mind is a healthy action when you know you're headed in the wrong direction.

CONSIDER THIS:

You said yes to some things when you were less busy, and those things may no longer fit your capacity.

You said yes to some things before you knew something better was coming along.

You said yes to some things before you clarified what was next.

You said yes to some things at the height of your people-pleasing phase.

You don't have commitment issues if you occasionally change your mind.

● ● ●

Everything you think isn't a fact. When you experience anxiety, what you think is often distorted and then bleeds into how you behave.

Thought: *"They are mad at me."*

Behavior: *You break your routine of saying "good morning" because you think people are mad at you.*

Thought: *"People don't get me."*

Behavior: *You isolate yourself.*

Notice your thoughts. Base your behavior on the facts that you can confirm, not on what you think based on fear.

Anxious thinking can be a habit, but you can break habits with practice.

●　●　●

S upport doesn't mean that someone always agrees with you. Instead, they have your best interest in mind. Your best interest could mean not agreeing with a bad decision.

If people always agree with you or never offer you feedback, it could be because they have found you to be sensitive to criticism.

In healthy relationships, we can do the following to better receive feedback:

▸ *Really listen to what is said.*

▸ *Resist the urge to be defensive and overprotect yourself.*

▸ *Sit with the information, and consider it carefully before rejecting it.*

▸ *Determine what you would like to do with the information.*

If someone tells you that you're frazzled, you can decide that you don't agree with their assessment. You can even decide that you love being frazzled. Or maybe you'll decide you want to appear more at ease in the world and choose to make a change. Ultimately, you get to decide what you want to do with someone else's feedback.

Invite honesty into your relationships.

● ● ●

Manipulation has long-term effects on your relationships. When someone can convince you to resist growth, limit yourself, and minimize your victories, their strategies become your strategies against yourself. When someone's voice lives inside your head, they can harm you even when they aren't present.

It can be helpful to wonder:

▸ *Are these thoughts coming from me, or did someone else plant this seed?*

▸ *What kind words do I need to say to myself?*

▸ *What were the other person's motives for creating this mental confusion within me?*

Some people think it's to their advantage to keep your self-esteem low.

Notice when the voice of others is taking over the voice in your head.

● ● ●

S ome people believe that those who are good at confrontation (difficult conversations) enjoy it. But it may just be that they're more practiced at these kinds of conversations and willing to have them despite the discomfort.

If you want to handle challenging conversations better, read more books and articles about communication. Lean toward understanding the other person. Be careful to avoid applying what didn't work in the past.

Confrontation doesn't require that you enjoy it. You simply need willingness, skill, and practice.

●   ●   ●

P rojection is a fascinating psychological phenomenon that occurs without our conscious awareness. It's when we attribute our emotions, thoughts, and actions to other people, as if they are responsible for them. It's like taking our inner world and projecting it onto the outside world, as if our own beliefs and behaviors belong to someone else.

Projecting is a powerful tool that keeps us from looking within. For example, you might think someone perceives you negatively when they don't at all. It's just a reflection of how you unconsciously see yourself.

The relief you need can be found within.

● ● ●

L oving yourself won't save you from people who seek to harm you.

Loving yourself won't save you from people not loving you back.

Hopefully, it will help you recognize unloving behaviors sooner, however.

Unhealthy relationships are not a reflection of low self-esteem and poor self-worth. You can love yourself and know your worth while still finding yourself in a bad relationship.

You deserve love. We all deserve love.

But loving yourself is not a prerequisite for being loved.

Practice loving yourself, but don't blame your mistreatment on not loving yourself enough.

● ● ●

Megan's mother, Sam, often gossiped about Megan's partner. The allegations were far-fetched and salacious. Once, Sam told family members that Megan was in an abusive relationship because she couldn't make her own decisions.

The truth was that Megan felt empowered in her relationship and had no issue speaking up for herself. On one occasion, Sam had asked to borrow money, and Megan said had no. Afterward, Sam started rumors about abuse.

Some people create narratives that support what they want to believe. Lying is their way of trying to be in control.

Unfortunately, you can't control the spread of gossip or lies about you.

● ● ●

You may struggle to distinguish between what's normal and what's healthy. Notice when you're trying to convince yourself and others that what has been normal for you is healthy.

Unhealthy norms can look like

▸ *A child waking their parents up for work because they overslept after a long night of drinking*

▸ *Doing your coworker's share of the work because you don't want them to get in trouble*

▸ *Yelling at your children daily because they upset you*

Unhealthy behaviors are normalized in an attempt to make the behaviors seem acceptable.

Something can happen routinely and still not be okay. Be willing to challenge unhealthy standards. Saying to yourself "This is not normal" can free you from rationalizing damaging patterns of behavior.

● ● ●

Narratives are a powerful tool that can hold you captive or free you.

Narrative therapy is an approach used by therapists that focuses on separating the individual from the problem. By externalizing their issues, people are able to gain a better understanding of their situation and take control of their lives. The therapy relies on the individual's own skills and sense of purpose to guide them through difficult times, rather than relying on external factors. This approach is empowering and can help individuals build a strong foundation for a happier, healthier life.

CONSIDER THIS:

What stories are you telling about yourself?
For example: *"I'm terrible at small talk."*

What stories do you find yourself repeating to others?

In the story, what are your limitations?
For example: *"Talking to new people feels weird."*

In the story, who is against you?

Does your story need to be revised?

Why would it be helpful for you to tell the story in a different way?
For example: *"If I engaged in more small talk, I could gain more connections at networking events and conferences."*

● ● ●

Hard truth: Some people intend to hurt you, bring you down, or create chaos.

Bad things happen to people who don't deserve it, and yes, it's unfair.

Trying to understand why something happened might get in the way of your healing from it. You may never know why. So feel what you need to feel without putting together the missing pieces.

Control what you can—specifically, your response.

●　●　●

T hat's what she gets," Dallas said after finding out that his ex-wife's new boyfriend cheated on her. After the long and chaotic divorce she put him through, he thought she deserved a dose of unhappiness.

Rejoicing in the pain of others is a sign of internal unhappiness, pain, and trauma. It isn't a healthy response. Even when others have upset us, we can have empathy.

Notice when you find pleasure in someone else's misery, and tend to the parts of yourself that need healing.

● ● ●

Notice when someone doesn't have your best interests at heart.

People who want the best for you won't encourage you to stay in unhealthy relationships.

People who want the best for you won't cosign bad ideas.

People who want the best for you will encourage you to make decisions that serve you.

People who want the best for you will not withhold praise.

Intentionally or unintentionally, some people may lead you in the wrong direction. It's your job to know when you shouldn't listen to the same person twice. It's your job to notice when the feedback doesn't fit your situation.

● ● ●

Trying to keep up with others is an exhausting job. You won't be able to achieve your goal for long, because the bar will always move. There will always be something new to acquire or to pretend to be.

Sometimes, we want something simply because someone else has it. When I was in college, a friend of mine got a new luxury car. I was driving a car that looked like a turtle. In fact, that's what I called it. So when she got her car, I thought, "I need one of these."

Ask yourself why you truly want something:

▸ *Is this something other people say I should want?*

▸ *Is this something that looks appealing because others have it?*

▸ *Is this something that could actually work for my lifestyle and who I am?*

▸ *Is this something that I want because it looks good?*

▸ *Is this really meant for me?*

Peace comes from acquiring only what truly brings you pleasure and meaning without living beyond your means.

● ● ●

When I sit with people in a therapeutic capacity, they often say things like "My dad was a heavy drinker," when their father was actually an alcoholic. They opt for softer language because saying the A-word is too hard. When we do this, we try to hide our pain through language.

The assumption is that softer words will keep us from coming undone by what happened to us. But sometimes, we need to come undone. A little unpacking is not a bad thing if it helps us acknowledge the truth of what happened. That's when healing truly begins.

Consider the terminology you use to describe the difficult times in your life, and ask yourself these questions:

▸ *How can I reshape these narratives to give them more meaning?*

▸ *If I were to write these stories down, would it be clear what happened to me, or would people only have a vague understanding of it?*

▸ *How can I use language to tell the whole story?*

● ● ●

I used to think play was immature. Even in middle school, I thought we were too grown to play video games.

Adults often tell themselves they don't have time to play, but we all need to *make* time for it.

Here are some ideas for adult play:

- *Play video games.*
- *Blow bubbles.*
- *Do crossword puzzles.*
- *Cook or bake for fun.*
- *Color, paint, or doodle.*
- *Make up a story.*
- *Try paintball.*
- *Spend time with friends.*

- *Garden.*
- *Spend time on a swing.*
- *Join a sports club.*
- *Play with Legos.*
- *Knit or sew.*
- *Dance.*
- *Go on an adventure.*
- *Try something new.*

● ● ●

Give yourself permission to not have everything figured out, regardless of your age.

"Quarter-life crisis" and "midlife crisis" are terms for the discomfort some people feel when their life isn't what they thought it would be.

Age isn't an indication of what you should know. It's freeing to be willing to learn, and it's brave to be willing to pivot.

• • •

We don't get to decide when we make a mistake, but we certainly get to decide how we respond.

Beating yourself up doesn't make anything better. Forgiving yourself for making a mistake is a beautiful practice.

Here are some ways to forgive yourself:

- *Recognize that you are not unique in your ability to make mistakes. Tell yourself:* **"This is part of being human. I will not always get it right."**

- *Take ownership of your mistakes. There's nothing worse than a person who denies their errors. When you deny them, you miss the opportunity to learn from them, and you make the additional mistake of being out of integrity.*

- *Accept that you can't control how others react to your mistake. People don't have to accept your apology, but you need to accept their choice.*

- *Give yourself some grace. Self-compassion matters.*

● ● ●

It's difficult to navigate relationships with family members who may have undiagnosed mental health issues. It isn't uncommon for people in this situation to resist help, instead placing blame on others for their problems.

When a loved one doesn't believe they need help, you will need help yourself to manage your feelings. You can't control the situation, and it's heartbreaking. Be sure to take care of yourself.

● ● ●

When you notice unhealthy patterns in a relationship, ask yourself:

▸ *What am I contributing to the dynamic?*

▸ *How is my upbringing affecting the relationship?*

▸ *Are my expectations reasonable for the other person?*

▸ *Am I holding the other person accountable for their behavior?*

Without effort, unhealthy patterns will not disappear. With effort, your relationships have the potential to improve.

● ● ●

People teach you from their own perspective. Some of their advice may be applicable for you, while some advice may never be for you at all.

While visiting family in Alabama, my uncle lectured me about how to kill a chicken. I have yet to use that skill. He found it very useful in his life, but it isn't useful in mine. This is an obvious example, but most of the time, you will have to use your discernment skills to determine what advice is useful for you. Set aside the rest.

Don't allow someone to influence you unless it makes sense to do so.

• • •

Tending to what you already have is the new "acquiring more."

Sometimes, you don't need more friends. You need to connect more with the ones you have.

Sometimes, you don't need a new relationship. You must practice valuable skills in the one that exists.

Sometimes, you don't need more stuff. You need to take care of the things you already possess.

CONSIDER THIS:

What existing thing needs your attention?

What do you need to take better care of?

What in your life requires deep maintenance?

Starting over won't cure issues with sustainability and poor maintenance. You can preserve the life and quality of what you already have.

● ● ●

There was a time when I thought I couldn't celebrate until others joined me. But the best celebrations in my life have been small.

Your victories, big or small, deserve a moment of pause and reflection with or without people cheering you on. When you're doing a lot, you may see your accomplishments as just another checkbox on a long list. But pause and praise yourself. Take yourself out on a date. Pause and say "thank you" to no one in particular. Sit with your achievements, and be in awe of yourself.

● ● ●

Contentment is not a matter of settling for less. It's a feeling of ease with what you have.

There's a time to strive and a time to be still.

Enjoying where you are is not complacency. It's recognizing that you have enough.

CONSIDER THIS:

What will it take for you to have enough?

Will the bar move once you reach that point, so that you feel you must have more?

Finding peace where you are is a practice.

● ● ●

Tasha sat on the sofa in my therapy office, crying about what she thought was one of the biggest mistakes in her life. She had purchased her first home and felt trapped. Mostly we sat together as I watched her cry.

Being a therapist has taught me to

▸ *Let people feel sad.*

▸ *Let people be angry.*

▸ *Let people grieve.*

I don't have to be comfortable while watching it, but I also don't have to intervene and stop them from processing their feelings.

If they can't feel their feelings with me, they will do it alone without support. Being there can be enough.

● ● ●

When Jesse met Ty in college, she just knew Ty was going to become someone special. Ty worked part-time, seemed ambitious, and had the support of loving parents. After five years of dating, however, Jesse did not see this potential realized. Ty still worked at the same company he had worked for in college, while Jesse was deeply goal-driven and couldn't understand Ty's lack of effort. Jesse wanted a stable future and had concerns that Ty was complacent in life.

Some people will not reach their potential.

You might see possibilities for someone that they don't see for themselves. Avery tried to convince her best friend, Melissa, that her cakes were good enough to sell. But Melissa never believed she could do it.

Waiting for someone to reach their potential could mean waiting a lifetime.

Focus on the person as they are, and resist creating a reality for them that doesn't exist.

● ● ●

Over-caring for others and under-caring for yourself is an unfortunate trend.

Notice your unmet needs, and consider how you're contributing to your neglect.

CONSIDER THIS:

Are you there for others in moments when you aren't mentally present for yourself?

Are you giving so much of yourself away that you're depleted?

Does it take a long time to recover after engaging with certain people?

What adjustments need to be made for you to take better care of yourself?

REMEMBER THIS:

Saving the world should never come at the cost of losing yourself.

● ● ●

S top waiting for everything to be "just right."

When I moved into my first apartment in college, I got a
Christmas tree and decorations during the holiday season.
I was single and didn't want to wait until I had a family to send
out cards and have a tree. I wanted my blue and silver tree that
year, so I created what I wanted.

We have to let go of what we thought was supposed to
happen, stop living in wait for what we hope is to come, and
start living in the present. Living in wait isn't living; it's putting
your life on pause.

●　●　●

C hoosing to do nothing is still a decision, even if it's a passive one.

When you can't decide, you are choosing to be in limbo.

When you don't speak up, you will likely reexperience something similar in the future.

Making a decision is assertive, while not deciding is passive.

Actively choose what you want and take action.

● ● ●

W e think people notice more about us than they do. We insist we can't wear the same outfit because people will remember. We agonize over such things, but they're inconsequential to others.

- *People have a lot of things to remember. Our brains can only hold so much, and your embarrassing moment will likely not make the cut.*

- *You are the main character of your story, not everybody else's story. Things that happen to you feel like a big deal, but that doesn't mean they're a big deal to others.*

- *Does it matter that you did something embarrassing in front of someone you don't know and will possibly never know?*

- *If you see the person on a regular basis, you have plenty of opportunities to create a different impression. If you meet your coworker for the first time with a stain on your shirt, you will have dozens more encounters with them. That first meeting will seem small in comparison.*

● ● ●

There is no appropriate rhythm to grief.

Grief happens moment to moment, not day to day. The world will move on around you, and people won't remember your loss. You will be different, but you don't have to overcome the loss in order to move forward. You will simply learn to live with it.

●　●　●

S tay close to people who check on you when they know
you're going through something.

A simple text saying "How are you?" means a lot.

A hug can make a big difference.

Remember this when someone you know is struggling. Your presence can go a long way.

Some people aren't clear enough about what they need to let others know. You can offer someone your support without clear directions from them.

● ● ●

I'm cautious about accepting help from people when their motive is to be able to brag about it to others.

I appreciate genuine acts of kindness, but not forced kindness for perception purposes only.

Some people are genuinely there for you, and some will want others to know how much they helped you. Be wary of insincere support.

• • •

S ometimes a solution isn't about trying harder; it's about
letting go.

As a gardener, I've tried to revive dead cucumber plants, herbs, and others by giving them more water or more light. But some things can't be revived.

Releasing can be a step forward.

Learn to distinguish between persistence and wisely letting go.

CONSIDER THIS:

Are you trying to revive something that can't survive?

Have you been passionate and bold in your efforts?

Will letting go make you feel like a failure?

Will you be able to live with letting this go?

● ● ●

E veryone feels angry at times. Anger is an emotion just like any other, and it's important that we allow ourselves to feel it, as long as we don't hurt anyone.

You may cross paths with people who take advantage of you or mistreat you. This may cause you to feel angry, which is a totally normal reaction. There's no reason to feel embarrassed or like you need to hide your hurt and anger.

Manage your anger in healthy ways:

- *You don't have to hold on to your anger. You can be angry in the moment and then let it go.*

- *Be aware of what triggers your anger.*

- *Set boundaries around your interactions with people so that you are less likely to be triggered by the same things.*

- *Get to the root of what causes your triggers. Maybe they are a sign of some work you need to do on yourself.*

- *Figure out how anger manifests in you, and come up with strategies for managing it.*

● ● ●

Ashley was at an impasse in her relationship with her boyfriend. She asked several friends what she should do. Some thought she should break up with him. Others thought she should work it out. This confused her because there were viable reasons to leave and viable ones to stay.

When you've been taught to listen to others, it can be hard to make a decision without validation from them.

Practice running things by others less often.

Practice feeling certain before sharing with others.

Practice making decisions for yourself that others may or may not validate.

This is your life to live. Do the heavy lifting when it comes to big decisions. No one else will have to deal with the consequences.

● ● ●

It's a lifelong learning process to become acquainted with who you are. After all, you are constantly learning and changing even if you don't realize it.

On average, I read about forty books a year. I love to read, and books have been my companion since childhood. When I share how many I read, some people say they'd like to read more. But reading for pleasure is not the same as having to read for school. People are uncomfortable acknowledging that they only read for utility purposes. But no one has to read unless they truly enjoy it.

Perhaps you don't like to try new things as much as you'd like to be seen as someone who wants to try new things.

Perhaps you don't like being in a group setting despite wanting to be more social.

Perhaps you are not as much of this or that as you'd like.

You are who you are, and you may not fit the ideal of who you'd like to be. But embracing who you truly are will simplify your journey in life.

Change is possible if it's what you really want to do. However, accepting yourself is freeing. Sometimes, becoming yourself is about simply allowing yourself to be as you are.

● ● ●

You will not always make the right choices. Self-forgiveness will grant you peace as you move forward.

Correcting your mistakes is growth.

Apologizing once you see you were wrong is growth.

Doing better is growth.

Remorse is growth.

● ● ●

My friend LaToya stopped answering my calls. I have no clue why. One day we were friends, and then we weren't. There was no explanation, only assumptions of what could have caused the rift. Within weeks, I decided to release her and stop thinking up stories about what happened. I will never know.

I wonder if we always deserve an explanation. I'm not sure that the other person believes we do, and when I've left relationships, I have also justified my decision for not offering an explanation. In some instances, my honesty about why I chose to end a relationship might be too harsh and raw.

Unexplained endings are tough.

The ending you deem necessary might not happen.

You may have to find a way to move forward without the closure you want.

● ● ●

In some relationships, we need a particular dynamic to shift. In these instances, we can use strategies to salvage the relationship without ending it. We can share boundaries. If we've already set boundaries, and the person still isn't getting it, we can try to shift the relationship in a way that allows for less.

We may want less

▸ *Conflict*

▸ *Gossiping*

▸ *Physical interaction*

▸ *Time spent*

▸ *Energy usage*

Pulling back from a relationship is not mean or spiteful. It's about showing up as your best self. Limiting your time with someone can allow you to be more fully present when you do show up for them. Doing less can be loving.

● ● ●

People often send mixed messages because they believe that if they're honest, they won't get what they want. When you're in a relationship with someone, it would be challenging to say "I really like spending time with you, but you're not the type of person I want to be with long-term." Or for an employer to tell their employees "This is a very demanding job. We expect you to work way into the evening and not spend a lot of time with your family. We really need you to be on call at all times." These are difficult things to say out loud!

In order to have more integrity in our communication and avoid mixed messages, we must be clear and provide a complete picture of what we want and need. We have to give people the option to hear our full truth and make a decision for themselves about moving forward.

People may not like what you have to say, but honesty gives them the freedom to choose. Be willing to allow people to walk away when what you want is not aligned with their needs.

• • •

My closest friends hold some of the same boundaries as me, so our connections are easy. Some people naturally agree with our boundaries because they are similar to us. Others disagree with our boundaries but still respect them. Then, there are folks who require special handling because they make placing boundaries into a workout.

People are unique, and your boundaries should fit your needs with them. Some people don't need firm restrictions, while others need clear limits.

CONSIDER THIS:

What people in your life generally respect boundaries?

Which people in your life make it challenging to set boundaries?

● ● ●

Years ago, I mistook a dream about someone as cause to reach out to them and rekindle a connection. I returned to what I'd left—a dysfunctional relationship that I could not fix. It wasn't long before I remembered why I had left and regretted going back.

You can miss someone and not desire to return to a relationship with them.

Maybe you miss the possibilities if the situation were different.

Maybe you miss some fond moments together.

Maybe you miss not having to explain their absence.

Maybe you miss parts of their personality.

Remember why it ended, and allow yourself to miss people who are no longer in your life, regardless of the reason.

● ● ●

Actual limitations are real and tangible barriers to achieving your goals. These can include financial constraints or physical limitations. They aren't excuses; they're real obstacles that you must work around or overcome to reach your goals.

Perceived limitations may not exist. They are often based on limiting beliefs or self-doubt, and they can hold you back from pursuing your dreams. For example, you might believe you need to be more intelligent to pursue a particular career or that you're too old to start a new hobby.

Be honest with yourself about what is truly holding you back from going after something you want. Take a step back, and ask yourself whether the limitation is based on fact or belief.

Even if you determine that the limitation is actual, don't give up on your dreams. Instead, look for ways to work around the limitations or find alternative paths to reaching your objectives.

● ● ●

The myth is that there isn't enough time. There is plenty of time. There isn't enough focus with the time you have. You win by directing your attention toward better things.

—James Clear, author of *Atomic Habits*

Time management is time allocation.

Notice when you're spending time with people who deplete you.

Notice when you need to ask for help instead of allowing for more time to figure it out alone.

Notice when you're engaged in distracting activities.

Doing one thing differently is a small step toward using your time wisely.

CONSIDER THIS:

What one thing can you do to improve how you allocate your time?

What are your biggest distractions?

• • •

When we see videos of babies learning to walk, the adults in the background are usually encouraging. "You can do it! Good job! Yay!" They don't say "Hurry up! Walk faster!"

Be gentle with yourself as you implement new practices. There's nothing to hurry toward. Take your time learning, and practice with patience and grace.

Progress does not look like mastery. It looks like slow growth.

● ● ●

Chasing people who don't reciprocate your feelings will leave you in a state of longing.

Move toward people who want you around and love you unconditionally. Spend more time with them, and grow deeper in those connections.

You will never be enough for some people, but you will be deeply loved by others. Sometimes, you might admire someone and confuse that with needing a relationship with them. Learn to admire people from afar and nurture the connections nearby.

Follow the love.

● ● ●

Having questions, doubts, or mixed feelings can be unsettling when we feel like we're supposed to know, but questioning can be healthy. Questioning aspects of our lives is a sign that we aren't complacent, and it shows that we are introspective. It's not necessarily a bad thing to wonder where different choices might lead you. We don't have to be clear and sure about every single thing.

• • •

In a loving relationship, release your defenses. Many of us carry wounds from past connections. Those wounds keep us protective and defensive, but this can prevent progress in relationships.

Practice listening without interrupting.

Practice wondering how the other person's truths are affecting the relationship.

Practice accepting things that might be hard to hear.

It might hurt to hear criticism, but it can be wise to listen.

● ● ●

R ob believed the food he made was too salty, and he was never sure how to properly cook meat. So he ate out most nights and gave up on learning how to cook.

No one starts learning to cook and instantly becomes a Michelin-starred chef. Even world-renowned chefs practice their skills and explore new recipes.

Failure and setbacks are a natural part of the learning process. If you give up too quickly, you miss out on opportunities for growth. You may allow for more fluctuations when you see learning as a practice.

Don't expect mastery when implementing a new boundary, changing your habits, or pursuing a new skill. Let it be a practice, and be patient.

● ● ●

I 've had clients who are very depressed or anxious, and they might tell me they've been crying every day for a month. At first glance, that might seem like a bad thing, but crying is communication. It can be helpful, leading us to talk about our problems and get help.

What a gift it is to be able to form tears and have emotional reactions to life. Our tears make us aware that something going on inside us needs to be discussed and processed. Our tears draw our attention so that we can get to the root of what caused them.

● ● ●

My neighbor Bina lived with her mother, Padma. When Padma died, Bina locked up her room. No one goes in, and nothing has been moved or cleaned since the death. It's been at least ten years. Even though the room is locked, Bina's pain seeps out in unconscious ways.

We can't lock grief away.

There can be some value in compartmentalizing, however. It's okay to tell yourself "I can't feel this at the moment, but at some point today, I'm going to allow myself the time and space to really feel the impact of this." Compartmentalization has to be temporary.

Don't make a habit of compartmentalizing your pain. The locks will eventually break, and the emotions will overflow.

● ● ●

Time doesn't cure pain, but it offers you space to develop your understanding, implement new ways to function, and experience new things.

When you stop rushing yourself to process your thoughts and emotions, you learn to stop rushing others.

Repeat After Me:

I'm not in a hurry.

I have time to process.

● ● ●

Let's say you tell someone you can't go to their party. As an excuse, you say your parents are going to be in town. Instead of getting the escape you were looking for, the person tells you to bring your parents. Now you're stuck going to a party with your parents, and you didn't even want to go in the first place. It wasn't that you didn't want to go to the party because your parents were coming; you just didn't want to go to the party. Period, the end.

Being clear and concise is more likely to get us the end result that we want, but so many of us still find ourselves overexplaining. This tendency is a symptom of pleasing people. We think that if we explain ourselves, it will soften whatever information we are sharing. We are trying to absorb any discomfort the person who is receiving our explanation may have, but more often than not, that doesn't work.

Furthermore, we cannot please everyone with our explanations. Our reasons may not be sufficient to everyone else, and they don't need to be. Sometimes I don't answer my phone, and I'm not doing anything that someone else would find particularly important. I may be folding clothes or watching something on TV. Those reasons may not feel valid to someone else, but the fact remains that I don't want to talk.

●　●　●

To remain humble, remember your past. Remember where you once were.

Being different from others does not mean you're better than them.

One path to compassion is remembering the old you who still had much to learn.

● ● ●

While watching a music awards show with friends, someone yelled, "She's too old to have her hair cut like that!" The person they were referring to was a middle-aged celebrity with an asymmetrical bob hairstyle.

What's the appropriate age for that hairstyle? I don't think there is one. Certainly, the person with that hairstyle didn't feel aged out of wearing it. My new goal is to be a ninety-year-old woman with a bob cut!

Age limits are commonly placed on us even when there is no limitation in sight. "I need a ranch-style home," my thirty-year-old friend said, because he assumed he'd have challenges with walking as he got older.

We age ourselves and others through language. Notice yourself using age-limiting language.

"Too young" and "too old" have been successfully challenged many times.

Age-related language is another way that we limit ourselves and others.

● ● ●

Sometimes, we listen to people with no expertise or experience because of their role in our life—partner, parent, sibling, best friend, etc.

Loving someone doesn't mean you have to follow their poor advice.

When you need good advice, go to someone with more experience with your issue.

Wise people will admit what they don't know.

Unwise people will provide answers even if they don't know what they're talking about.

● ● ●

You may not understand what someone is going through, so in those moments, it's best to listen.

You won't have a reference point for every human experience. Don't force yourself to relate when you can simply listen and learn.

• • •

I nhabit your life.

Pay more attention to yourself.

You deserve a lot of attention, so focus your gaze inward.

● ● ●

Your energy and excitement level tell you what you enjoy, what makes you feel at ease, and what bothers you.

Listen to your feelings. It's how you discover more about yourself.

Your feelings are clear:

▸ *"I don't feel comfortable in this situation."*

▸ *"This feels forced; I don't want to do it anymore."*

▸ *"I'm at ease when I'm at home with my family."*

Follow your feelings.

● ● ●

R eal estate moves swiftly during certain seasons. When I was ready to buy my first home, I took my time to decide on the best fit. Since I didn't rush, others made offers on some of the homes I'd viewed, which meant they were no longer available when I was ready.

Opportunities can come and go quickly. When you delay action, you might miss the chance to capitalize on something.

Things won't always happen on your timetable. Be ready to move swiftly when you want something—and be willing to accept that sometimes the timing won't be right.

● ● ●

You can communicate well in some relationships and not others. Communication skills are unique to the individuals in the relationship. Therefore, your skills are not universal and applicable to everyone.

For example, you may communicate effectively at work but have challenges in your relationship with your parents.

When you're parenting, each child might listen to feedback differently. We have to be flexible and try different communication styles.

Adapt your style to the people involved.

● ● ●

When we learn to protect ourselves at an early age, it can be hard to recognize the difference between boundaries and walls. Healthy boundaries allow the right people in while keeping unhealthy relationships out. Walls, on the other hand, keep everyone out.

We might say "I've always had to protect myself" without noticing when self-protection is no longer needed. We negatively impact our relationships when we overuse expired skills.

When significant people show us that they can't be there for us, it can be hard to believe anyone ever will. But when people consistently care for us, it's an opportunity for us to heal by loving and trusting them.

Are you building walls or creating healthy boundaries?

●　●　●

Life isn't fair. You may have to take care of things that are not your responsibility. Even when things are your responsibility, it might feel like too much.

Here are some key ways to manage your resentment:

▸ *Notice what grinds your gears. Please don't ignore it.*

▸ *Talk about what is unlikely to improve.*

▸ *Get angry, because holding in your anger isn't helpful.*

▸ *Grieve what needs to be grieved.*

▸ *Be clear about what bothers you.*

▸ *Think back on the stories you still carry about how you were wronged.*

Ignoring problems builds resentment, while acknowledging them can release resentment. Sometimes, the only change you can make in a situation is a shift in your perspective.

• • •

Some people who come to you for advice don't really want your advice. They want you to agree with what they've already decided. When you notice this pattern, remove yourself as the advice giver, and simply listen.

● ● ●

When I moved to a new city, I sought connections as deep as the ones I'd created with my old friends. I overlooked the time and effort it took me to cultivate those old friendships. I wanted a deep connection instantly with the new people, but those kinds of connections take time.

Friendships will have varying degrees of closeness. You will engage with some people daily and others only occasionally. You can be close with multiple friends, and you don't have to have a "best friend." Recognize each relationship on its own terms.

● ● ●

I'm learning not to chase people who don't desire a healthy relationship.

I'm learning not to chase dreams that others want me to pursue.

I'm learning not to chase things that look good for others but aren't for me.

I'm learning not to chase.

What's meant for me will come to me without applied pressure.

• • •

Sometimes, our bad days don't have anything to do with what is going on outside ourselves. It's not about the day, or what anybody has done; it's us. Sometimes, it's our hormones. Sometimes, we are emotionally exhausted. Sometimes, we just wake up feeling grumpy. We have to be able to recognize when our energy has shifted; otherwise, we'll walk through life blaming other people.

We may also notice that there are certain circumstances, situations, or people that trigger our bad days. Maybe after interacting with certain people, having a certain kind of day at work, or a particularly challenging parenting moment, we feel off.

To preserve your relationships when you're having a bad day, you can

- **Let people know how you're feeling.** *You can tell the people around you that you're not in the best mood, or that you may be a little quiet.*

- **Apologize quickly.** *If you end up losing your temper, let people know you weren't your best self, and acknowledge your behavior.*

- **Reach out for support.** *Often when you're going through something, you think keeping to yourself is for the best, but isolation is not the answer.*

● ● ●

Surprisingly, first therapy sessions are usually a relief. After holding things in for years, people let words spill out, and tears flow. Letting emotions release feels like unclogging a drain.

When you hold on to your experiences, thoughts, and emotions without sharing them with others, you miss the opportunity to process and integrate them fully. Sharing with others can help you gain perspective, feel supported, and receive feedback that can aid in your growth.

Sharing your story with others reduces feelings of isolation and loneliness. When you open up about your experiences, you permit others to do the same. You may find that you have more in common with others than you initially thought.

While sharing your story can be a powerful tool for healing and growth, it's essential to do so in a safe and supportive environment. Choose people who will validate your feelings and experiences without judgment.

● ● ●

R ecognize the difference between correcting someone respectfully and constructively versus doing so in a confrontational or aggressive way. Perhaps when shopping with a friend, you might say "Would you like to try that in another color?" rather than "That looks bad on you."

People can accept loving feedback, but they will dismiss a mean or aggressive comment. It's essential to communicate with empathy.

● ● ●

Wanting less and pulling back from a relationship are not about being mean or spiteful—they're really about showing up as our best selves. It's much better to have a workout when you feel good and your body is rested than one when you didn't sleep well, your mind's all over the place, and you can barely lift your arms. Likewise, pulling back from a relationship can allow us to be more fully present when we do show up for that person. Doing less can be loving.

● ● ●

Sharing can happen incrementally, on varying levels, or not at all. I saw an article about a celebrity who "secretly" gave birth to her first child. Several months later, the public found out about it. There was no secret. We, the public, are not in her inner circle and not privy to certain areas of her life. We know the celebrity as an actress on a show; we don't know her personally.

Privacy is not secrecy. It's a healthy boundary to let people know about you according to who they are and the health of your relationship with them.

CONSIDER THIS:

Share limited information.

Share with some people on a need-to-know basis.

Withhold information when people have ill intentions.

Restrict your responses when people want more information than you feel comfortable sharing.

Indulge in deep conversations with people who demonstrate through their words and actions how much they care.

Be open with those who are committed to your wellness.

Share freely with people who honor your privacy.

● ● ●

I once had a friend who had a friend who just wasn't my type of person. However, this friend of a friend really wanted to be my friend. She would ask to go for coffee and spend time together and all but ask me "How come I'm not your friend?" I couldn't really explain it. There wasn't anything wrong with her. There wasn't anything in particular that she had done. She just wasn't for me.

Not being on the same page or wanting the same things inside of our relationships can make us uncomfortable. This discomfort can be triggered by

▸ *Someone not being pleased with our actions*

▸ *Disagreeing with someone*

▸ *Not being aligned on the type of relationship you want*

▸ *Having to say a hard thing that someone else may not receive well*

▸ *Not being forgiven*

▸ *Being forgiven by someone who still isn't interested in continuing the relationship*

We sometimes try to fight this discomfort by forcing our perspective and preferences on others. Rather than accepting that this person is entitled to feel the way that they feel, we try to convince them of our point of view. When someone doesn't want to go to a function with us, we may have to get comfortable going alone. When someone isn't ready, or is unwilling, to forgive us, we may have to make our peace with being unforgiven. Our work is not to try to change their mind.

● ● ●

When something in your life falls apart, there's freedom in letting go.

When we hold on to something that needs to be released, we suffer.

When something shifts naturally, release it.

Repeat After Me:

I can't keep everything and everyone.
Shedding is a natural part of growth.

• • •

We often rush through life and focus only on the big picture, ignoring the little things that make life meaningful. Small details add value to our lives.

Notice the intricate details.

Be in your life fully to get the most out of it.

Immerse yourself in your experience of living.

Some small details I notice:

▸ *My monstera plant has a new leaf.*

▸ *The wound on my leg is healing.*

▸ *I have a new mole on my cheek in the middle of my dimple.*

CONSIDER THIS:

What are some small details that you notice about your life?

What gets in the way of your existing deeply in your life?

● ● ●

Everything doesn't happen for a reason. I wish it did. Then we could prevent some things from happening.

But we can't plan for everything. That makes life both beautifully mysterious and scary.

When you search for a reason for everything, it can leave you stuck.

Accept that life can be unfair, and some things happen without meaning. It's brave to keep going without having all the answers.

● ● ●

When you feel the urge to check out, check *in* instead. In other words, go inward.

Running away will leave behind unfinished business that will eventually show up again.

Distractions plug holes temporarily, but they don't improve our ability to manage, prevent, or tolerate discomfort, a crisis, or challenging times.

Leaning out is avoidance. Leaning in is problem-solving.

● ● ●

E xploring what you want is how you learn what you're willing to commit to.

Sometimes, you start and realize you are doing something for the wrong reason.

Sometimes, you start and need more motivation to finish something you're lukewarm about.

Sometimes, you stop something simply because it was a bad decision.

Sometimes, you start something and discover it isn't what you expected.

Sometimes, it's better to move on.

● ● ●

Everyone is annoying to someone else at some point. You annoy people, and they will annoy you. Let's normalize being annoyed and annoying as a part of being human.

My children yell, "She's being annoying!" I lament, "You are also annoying sometimes."

Notice what annoys you about others, and consider if you have those same tendencies at times.

● ● ●

Being active in your life means taking an intentional and engaged approach to how you live.

This can look like

▸ *Nurturing meaningful connections with family, friends, or colleagues by investing time and effort into building strong, supportive relationships*

▸ *Distinguishing between helping, harming, and being in the way of what others want for themselves*

▸ *Using your time to pursue things that match your values*

▸ *Accepting hard truths, feeling your feelings, and understanding that you can't force something to happen*

Some people fail to guide their lives. They exist, react, or escape.

Refuse to be that way. Be present instead.

● ● ●

It isn't healthy to not need others.

We need less independence and more community care.

More calling to check on people to see how they're doing.

More processing our day with others instead of holding it all in.

More celebrating with others and less keeping to ourselves.

Make more requests to connect with others instead of spending time alone.

●　●　●

On the brink of losing her mother, Sydney became a new mother herself. While she grieved and processed her sadness, her baby made her feel happy.

You will be sad about some things no matter how much healing happens. You don't have to be okay with everything that has happened to you. Feeling sad doesn't have to stop you from living, and you can feel sad and happy at the same time. Sadness moves with you, along with all of the other emotions you experience.

Choosing to feel more than one emotion at the same time will bring you freedom.

● ● ●

D iscipline is built with practice. Build discipline by challenging yourself more often.

A few ideas:

▸ *Go to bed thirty minutes earlier.*

▸ *Stretch for five minutes.*

▸ *Read before bed.*

▸ *Drink water as your sole beverage of choice.*

▸ *Write in a journal.*

● ● ●

M ost of us should use the phrase "It isn't for me" more often.

For example:

▸ *A bigger house? "It isn't for me."*

▸ *A smaller house? "It isn't for me."*

▸ *A pet? "It isn't for me."*

▸ *A short haircut? "It isn't for me."*

May you stop trying to impress others by doing anything that isn't "your thing."

● ● ●

S ome people who appear happy online are not satisfied in
real life.

Some people who appear to have it all together don't.

Some people who appear to be living the dream aren't.

Some people share only what makes them look their best.

CONSIDER THIS:

What do you portray to others that isn't true?

● ● ●

In an Instagram poll, I asked people what they assumed about me. The responses were mostly inaccurate. My social media posts feature my words, projects, and a small bit of my hobbies. However, people speculated about my parenting and relationships.

From time to time, it can be helpful to wonder "What assumptions am I making?"

Assumptions can seem like the truth when we want to believe them.

But remember when something isn't confirmed, it may not be true.

Ways to assume less:

▸ *Ask questions.*

▸ *Share your feelings.*

▸ *Lead with facts.*

● ● ●

I s it possible to live with no regrets?

It's more likely to live with manageable regrets. When we make a choice, we can't be certain we have made the right one. So, mistakes are inevitable.

Regret springs from guilt.

Regret springs from not living fully.

Regret springs from living inauthentically.

Intentional living might lead to fewer regrets, but it won't completely eliminate them.

● ● ●

E arly on, when I thought of an idea, I shared it immediately. After hearing feedback from others, I noticed that I often lost my belief in my own ideas. Now, when I'm passionate about a project, I share it with only a few people or sometimes not at all until I'm already going full steam ahead.

The questions that others pose can cause us to question ourselves.

CONSIDER THIS:

Keep some of your ideas to yourself.

The what-ifs that people throw out can discourage you.

The idea is merely your rough draft. It will be better understood when it's final.

• • •

L earn to care less about what won't matter for long.

You can practice today by asking:

▸ *Will this matter tomorrow?*

▸ *Will this matter in a month?*

▸ *Will this matter in a year?*

▸ *Will this matter in five years?*

Notice how long you're consumed by something that might not be as consequential as you think.

• • •

K ids are not the only ones who don't like to be told no. Adults also want to get what they want. Hopefully, with time, practice, and maturity, we become more accepting when we can't have what we want.

It hurts when people tell us no, but it's good for them to have boundaries.

Even when someone's boundaries are hard to hear, respect them.

● ● ●

S top giving up because you don't instantly understand
something or do it well.

It isn't a reasonable expectation that you will be immediately
good at something.

Acquire a taste for temporary discomfort on the path of
mastering something challenging.

● ● ●

I n the acknowledgments section of *Set Boundaries, Find Peace,* I thanked some folks and not others. A family member asked, "Why didn't you put my name in the back of the book?" Honestly, I didn't have anything to thank them for with respect to my career or who I am as a person.

Entitlement is believing you deserve something that hasn't been earned.

Sometimes, people feel entitled to other people's time.

Sometimes, people feel entitled to other people's resources.

Sometimes, people feel entitled to take up space in someone's life.

Titles (mother, father, sister, brother, boss, best friend, etc.) don't give the relationship meaning.

Deeds, time, and effort are what gain us a place in someone else's life.

Never allow your title to make you think you deserve something.

Relationships take work.

Ask Yourself:

▸ *What have I put into this relationship?*

▸ *How do they feel about the connection?*

● ● ●

Loneliness is cured by deepening your relationships with yourself and others. Vulnerability, consistent communication, intentional listening, and care will help you go deeper.

If you change nothing, your relationships or lack thereof will remain the same.

If you want to relieve loneliness, be intentional in your relationships.

● ● ●

▸ *"My sister won't forgive me for what I did when I was using."*

▸ *"I apologized to my daughter-in-law about what I said to other family members about her."*

▸ *"My life is in a better place now, and I'm ready to repair the relationships with my adult children."*

There are no do-overs, only apologies and hopes for forgiveness.

Sometimes, you can repair a relationship, but other times, you can't.

"Everyone deserves a second chance" is a choice-based statement. Not everyone believes it.

Second chances aren't guaranteed.

●　●　●

Whenever Josh and Issac argued, Josh would walk away and Issac would pursue him incessantly. Josh requested space to process his feelings before returning to the conversation.

For Issac, space was offensive and should never be tolerated. He wanted to work through issues immediately.

Learn to sit with the discomfort of not being liked or of someone else's anger. Trying to control how others respond will limit your ability to be honest in your communication. Healthy communication isn't always pleasing others with what you say.

Repeat After Me:

I cannot control other people's emotional reactions.

• • •

P eople who don't want to listen will often say you haven't explained yourself enough.

It can be frustrating when others don't seem to listen to you, and you might assume it means you didn't communicate your message effectively. But some people just don't want to listen.

It won't be effective to simply repeat yourself to someone who is bent on ignoring you. You cannot rephrase, restate, or get creative enough with your words to convince someone who doesn't want to hear what you say.

Understand the difference between saying enough and overexplaining, and don't waste your energy on someone who refuses to be receptive to your message.

● ● ●

R elationships are meant to teach you, help you unlearn what is no longer needed, and expand your thinking.

If you are moving further away from yourself in a relationship, repeating unhealthy habits, or stuck in damaging thinking:

▸ *Perhaps the relationship is not suitable for either person's needs.*

▸ *Perhaps you are refusing to change your practices.*

▸ *Perhaps you haven't been intentional about cultivating healthy relationships.*

Without sufficient practice in building healthy relationships, we sometimes repeat unhealthy cycles.

Relationships are a teaching tool. The more intentional your practice, the better they will become.

● ● ●

Thoughts for Highly Productive People:

▸ *Your worth is not measured by how much you finish on your to-do list.*

▸ *People aren't watching you as closely as you assume, so slow down.*

▸ *You will only complete some things on your list, and there will always be more to do.*

Success in productivity is knowing that you can't do it all.

● ● ●

G uilt-tripping is a common strategy people use to get their needs met.

People don't always manipulate us with the intention of being mean or deceitful. They do it because they want to get their way. At some point or another, we all manipulate someone else.

Manipulation becomes a problem when it's a pattern. From time to time, a person may say something like "I really wish you could come to my party. I'm so sad you can't make it," which is an expression of how they truly feel. However, if they say that every single time, it becomes a pattern of manipulation.

When someone never lets you have a boundary, it disrupts the relationship. You are likely to place distance between yourself and that person because it's no longer a safe space.

People learn to stop guilt-tripping when they see that their methods are no longer effective. Stop allowing manipulation to work.

It's crucial to consider integrity and respect when we try to get our needs met.

● ● ●

L iving a brave life rather than a safe life will make you proud of yourself.

Life is meant to be lived, which means everything can't go as planned.

Life is meant to be lived, which means not everything will come easily.

Life is meant to be lived, which means some of your decisions for yourself won't make others happy.

● ● ●

Sometimes, you want support but don't know how to ask, or you don't know how to accept help when it's offered. Managing your needs all by yourself works in some cases, but it isn't an effective strategy all the time.

CONSIDER THIS:

What messages do you tell yourself that keep you from asking for support?

● ● ●

Trying is a risk; living is a risk. Therefore, you are already living at risk. Nothing is guaranteed, and success can only be achieved if you try.

You can be afraid and press forward at the same time.

• • •

After you stand up for yourself, you might feel guilty. It doesn't mean you did anything wrong. Guilt will (and does) subside when you start to believe it's okay to speak up on your own behalf.

If you feel guilty, ask yourself:

▸ *Did I do something wrong?*

▸ *Have I harmed anyone?*

▸ *Where does my guilt come from?*

Guilt is a tricky emotion, because you have to discern if you truly did something wrong or if you were simply taught that you shouldn't do something that's actually reasonable.

● ● ●

N othing stunts our growth more than being unwilling to learn or try something new.

You might see trying something new as a risk, but never changing is also a risk.

Changes will happen whether you move with them or fight against them.

CONSIDER THIS:

What natural changes are you resisting?

When presented with new information, do you instantly dismiss it or consider it?

● ● ●

W̲e evolve within our relationships. This includes partnerships, parent-child relationships, and friendships. Our roles shift and change. Some shifts feel huge and significant, while others are subtle.

In long-term relationships with family and friends, you have to

- **Give people the space to become who they are.** *This is healthy. One of the most important things you will do in life is figure out who you are. Over the course of a relationship, however, we become different versions of ourselves.*

- **Recognize that in the life of a relationship, you and the other person may drift apart and then back together again and again.** *Life's transitions and shifts will cause a natural ebb and flow inside a relationship. Shifts don't mean the relationship has to end. Honor where you are in the relationship, and give it room to take on a new shape.*

- **Understand that people are not going to stay who they were when they were twelve, sixteen, or any other age.** *We create a lot of tension when we hold on to who someone used to be. It prevents us from appreciating who they are now.*

● ● ●

People are sometimes unaware of the harm they cause others. You aren't obligated to let their mistreatment go unremarked. Letting them know how they've wounded you can help them do better—and might save your relationship.

We prevent people from addressing their issues when we pretend they don't have any.

Holding people accountable is an excellent way to care for yourself and others.

● ● ●

In most cases, we create boundaries to preserve our relationships.

When someone is unwilling to respect a boundary, it can seem like boundaries aren't possible in that relationship. It's true that some people can't seem to respect limitations. Instead, they take them personally.

But it's even more important to set boundaries in complex relationships. When you do, you have to decide if you're ready for the possible consequences.

Remember that boundaries are about creating peace, not chaos.

● ● ●

There is no such thing as a perfect person; even the most well-intentioned people will love and disappoint us at times. People can't be themselves when there's an expectation of being perfect.

Acceptance comes from knowing that people make mistakes.

Love people while making space for what you don't like about them.

• • •

We may fear being honest with ourselves because we believe honesty is synonymous with action. But honesty is step one. We choose to stay as we are or change.

Sometimes, we aren't ready to leave a situation or change something about ourselves. Be patient with your process.

● ● ●

Relationships are your greatest teacher.

A few things I've learned from being in relationships with others:

▸ *I show up with my own baggage.*

▸ *My assumptions are usually wrong.*

▸ *People can love you and still not be everything you need.*

CONSIDER THIS:

What have you learned about yourself through your relationships?

● ● ●

B rutal honesty can sometimes mean cruel words.

Yes, it's important to be honest, but some people cannot handle the truth. When you decide to be honest, be mindful of the sensitivity of the other person.

● ● ●

L etting go of the fight to change people is not the same as giving up on them. When you let go, you acknowledge your inability to make people and situations into something they are not.

When someone says they aren't open to changing for you, believe them, and accept it.

You get to decide whether to keep them in your life.

● ● ●

S ome people won't apologize, and there's nothing you can do to change that.

Being accountable for our actions or lack of actions is hard, and some people can't or don't want to see themselves in an imperfect way.

Move forward without waiting for others to release you. Moving forward does not mean you ignore what happened. Instead, you decide to not allow it to occupy further space in your mind and consume everything else in your life. When you move forward, you can choose how and if you want to continue in the relationship.

● ● ●

H elping out of obligation or self-induced pressure builds resentment in relationships.

Sometimes, it's best to allow people to figure out their own solutions rather than to show up begrudgingly.

● ● ●

So many things test our resolve when it comes to the lessons and skills we have learned and are learning. One time I went to Home Depot to buy a plastic tub for my laundry room. The attendant at the store put it in my car, and when I got home, I realized they'd accidentally given me a set of eight tubs instead of just one. I was with someone who told me I should sell the extras. I don't know who I would have sold them to, but the Old Me would have figured it out. The Old Me would not have taken the extra tubs back to Home Depot, which I did. I thought to myself, "Ha! This is a test."

The Old Me is still in there. It's like there's Old Nedra on one shoulder and New Nedra on the other. I mostly side with New Nedra, but not always. Sometimes Old Nedra wins! We are not always 100 percent the best version of ourselves. So when we find ourselves slipping into those old habits, it's really important that we give ourselves grace. We have to remember to talk to ourselves in a loving way despite the fact that we said or did the wrong thing.

Growth is not always saying the right thing. Growth is also being aware of our mistakes and taking steps to course-correct when necessary.

Sometimes we want to forget ourselves—who we used to be and what we used to do. We don't want anyone else to know, because we think they will either judge us or diminish us. When I tell people about some of my hot-mess moments, they can hardly believe it, but that's who I was, and that's still part of who I am. That honesty doesn't take anything away from who I've become.

The Old You and the New You are both you. Leave space for all of yourself.

● ● ●

Whenever Kelly became upset with her father's aggressive tone and confrontational style, he would say, "That's how I am." Despite the impact on his relationships, he decided to remain the same, and others had to accept and deal with him as he was.

Unlearn that you must stay as you are because it's all you know. At some point, you choose to change or remain the same.

REMEMBER THIS:

When you choose change, it's because the old you no longer fits your current life.

Your old ways may no longer be useful.

You can't live in the past and the present.

Change is inevitable whether you choose to embrace it or not.

When your old habits no longer fit who you are or what you want for yourself, pivot.

● ● ●

You are allowed to feel sad. It's not the most comfortable feeling, but one that's needed. There's no such thing as feeling happy all the time. When something sad happens, you don't have to move to the brighter side swiftly.

Allow yourself to feel the sadness, and allow others the same courtesy.

Moving away from an experience too soon robs you (and others) of releasing the feelings.

• • •

If you want someone to stop offering you advice, you will likely have to have an uncomfortable conversation requesting that they stop.

If you stay passive, the person will continue to offer you unwanted advice.

And you must repeat yourself if someone doesn't listen the first time.

● ● ●

Personal growth is terrific, but it can affect your relationships in positive or negative ways. Some people welcome the changes you make, while others won't be open to seeing you differently.

Know this: It's normal for some people to have an issue with the "new you." You may need to curate new relationships for the person you've become.

● ● ●

K eeping it all in" is toxically rewarded with praise such as "You're strong," "You're so brave," and "You handle things well." Praising a lack of emotional expression encourages people not to feel their feelings.

Feeling and coming undone are healthy and courageous. Reclaim your innate privilege to be a human being with feelings. Bottling them up may have once been a survival skill, but it isn't a thriving skill.

Learn to let go of skills that were once for survival but that are now keeping you from self-connection, as well as connection with others.

● ● ●

B e generous, but keep something for yourself.

You are not to be constantly consumed by others.

Taking care of yourself means learning to keep parts of yourself safe.

Taking care of yourself means saying no in order to meet your needs.

Taking care of yourself means giving to others while also allowing yourself to be abundant.

● ● ●

S eeking to have a relationship that requires no work is an unreasonable expectation.

Whether they're romantic, platonic, or familial, maintaining relationships requires effort and communication. Conflicts and uncomfortable conversations are normal.

Avoiding difficult conversations or brushing issues under the rug may seem easier in the short term, but it can lead to resentment and further problems.

Understand that peace and growth are on the other side of uncomfortable conversations.

● ● ●

C hanging at any time is the right time. Many make resolutions at the top of the year and stop committing after a few months. Planning to do something for an entire year seems too long for some of us. We give up sooner than we'd like to.

Perhaps envisioning yourself seasonally, monthly, or even daily would work better for you.

This season:

▸ *I am creating and honoring myself. I am engaging in joyful collaborations and connections, and I'm enjoying life.*

● ● ●

S uppressing and dismissing your feelings might lead you to
believe you can feel without processing them. When you slow
down and feel your feelings, it will seem like you're feeling too
much too often.

Allow yourself to feel without putting yourself on a timeline.
Some pain takes years to process, while some takes days.

You will be processing something most of the time.

Practice allowing your feelings to come up without pushing
them down.

●　●　●

The things you pretend not to care about may be what you care about most deeply.

"I don't care" can mean:

▸ *I don't know how to express my feelings.*

▸ *It hurt, but I didn't want it to.*

▸ *I'm indifferent.*

▸ *I'm still figuring out what I feel.*

Tune in to yourself and what truly matters when no one is looking. Acknowledging that you care can be the first step toward growth.

● ● ●

How many of us have said we'd never do something, based on a negative story we heard on TV or from a friend? Whether it's a fear of flying, or fear of getting divorced, or fear of taking a new job across the country for a fresh start, we can become biased against new experiences simply based on a narrative we've heard from others.

Before you allow someone else's experience to stop you from doing something, consider the following:

- *Where is the anxiety coming from? Does it belong to you, or is it coming from someone else?*

- *Is the source reputable? What do you know about the person sharing their experience?*

- *Did you get the whole story? Are you basing your fear on a piece of the story?*

- *How can you create a different experience for yourself? What plan can you put in place to affect a different outcome?*

We hear horror stories from other people's lives and sometimes assume their hardship will become our own, but the way one person experiences something doesn't have to be our experience. We are all different. Our perspective is different. The way we handle stress is different. What is true for one person doesn't have to be true for us.

● ● ●

Accepting that some people won't like you no matter how great you are or how much good you do will free you to bask in the energy of those who do appreciate you.

Pursuing the admiration of everyone is an unwise use of your energy.

● ● ●

S ometimes it is healthy for us to take breaks from relationships, to pause. Stepping away is not the same as shutting down. Detaching is not the same as leaving. This need for separation happens a lot in friendships and family relationships. It can be harder in romantic situations, but there are times when we need to take a step back from a relationship.

This break can serve as a reset. It can allow us to figure out where we are and allow us to come back to the person with clearer expectations. We can also take that time to decide how we want to show up in the relationship.

● ● ●

People will create an entire story about how a situation played out, omitting the parts in which they did something to damage the relationship.

Editing the truth is how some people manage to live with themselves.

Accountability means admitting you messed up, which can be hard to acknowledge. People blame others because the truth is hard to live with.

It isn't your job to edit, redact, or change the parts that were left out. But sometimes, you have to live with people who choose to remember only one side of the story.

Healthy relationships are a sign of success.

Creating loving relationships is an intentional practice.

Receiving love requires openness.

Receiving love requires giving love.

Some people are still learning how to create healthy relationships. Be gentle with yourself as you apply new skills that may not have been modeled for you. Be patient with yourself as you develop the ability to be healthier in your relationships.

● ● ●

You can convince yourself that you don't need things you don't have. But lies you tell yourself as a means of protection are still lies.

You might convince yourself:

▸ *I don't need anyone to love me.*

▸ *I can do it on my own.*

▸ *I don't want to be in a relationship.*

CONSIDER THIS:

What lies have you told yourself because the truth is hard to accept?

What are you missing that you've convinced yourself you don't need?

● ● ●

I t's challenging to hear what others think about us without becoming defensive. Even when the comment is positive, it can still be hard to receive. When someone pays us a compliment, we often look for a way to deflect it. When someone offers criticism, we look for a way to deny it. We have a tendency to protect ourselves even when it's unnecessary.

● ● ●

N o longer completing the tasks you don't "have to" do is a way of empowering yourself.

"Have to" doesn't always mean we truly have to do something.

Make a list of what you believe you "have to" do. Consider whether some, or perhaps even all, are actually a choice.

"Have to" can be a sign that you're forcing yourself into a role that doesn't fit.

CONSIDER THIS:

What are you choosing to do?

What are you forcing, and what's been forced on you?

What can you choose for yourself?

● ● ●

It's emotionally immature to assume that our problems are greater than someone else's based on how their life looks from the outside. What you see isn't necessarily a reflection of their internal experience. Obstacles can motivate some people to change their circumstances, while others may feel paralyzed by them.

You cannot assume the weight of someone else's suffering.

● ● ●

When someone makes a mean comment, correct the behavior in the moment or soon after. When mistreatment is ignored, unwanted behaviors continue.

Sometimes, people aren't aware of how they come across. Let them know when you want them to change their delivery.

Seven ways to respond to a mean comment:

▸ *"I don't like the way you said that."*

▸ *"I want you to be assertive. But please choose your words carefully, and be mindful of your tone."*

▸ *"I want to make sure I'm responding appropriately. Can you clarify what you meant?"*

▸ *"That felt mean."*

▸ *"Please don't speak to me that way."*

▸ *"That sounds loaded. Is there something deeper we need to discuss?"*

▸ *"That sounded mean, so is there a different way to phrase what you said? Let's try it again."*

Letting it go is a gateway to resentment.

● ● ●

When you share with someone and they don't seem to be a good listener, don't give up on expressing how you feel. There may be someone else who listens better.

Not being a good listener doesn't make someone a bad person. It just makes them a poor listener.

Listening is a skill. Some people haven't acquired the skill to listen well.

● ● ●

Y our partner will not be all things.

Your best friend will not be all things.

Your parents will not be all things.

You will not be all things to everyone.

Learn to accept the fact that no one is all things to everyone.

We spread people too thin by expecting them to satisfy all our needs.

● ● ●

Be kind, and give people the benefit of the doubt. You have no clue what's happening behind their masks.

No one is at their best all the time, and you can't know why someone may be functioning at less than their best.

● ● ●

H ard truth: Some people are the reason for their own broken and unhealthy relationships. They don't see themselves in their troubles. They are ignorant to their patterns, so they point fingers at others while their relationships all have the same ending.

• • •

You are not required to explain anything, but in some instances, it's reasonable to offer more information.

You are not required to explain anything, but it can be kind in some circumstances.

You are not required to explain anything, but in some instances, it can be an example of healthy communication.

Discern when to offer more information and when to keep it short.

• • •

From now on, seek to meet people who are self-aware or willing to work on themselves.

Life is too short to repeat old patterns with new people. You deserve better.

● ● ●

When I tell people how many books I read, I often hear "I want to read more" or "I should read more," and my first question is always, "Do you like to read?" People often say that they don't, so then why would they say they want to read more?

We pressure ourselves to do things because they sound good, or because someone we consider influential has done something in a particular way and we want to emulate them. What we really need to think about is what works for us. In order for something to work for us, it has to be something we can sustain, and that can't happen if we're not actually invested in it. Most of us can read a book every week, but if you don't actually like to read, will you still be reading it by the end of the week or the month?

This doesn't just apply to habits that we're trying to pick up. In relationships, we need to think about our needs, preferences, likes, and dislikes. We have to dig into our own values, not just be reliant on what our parents say, or what our friends think, or what someone on the internet is doing.

Part of the reason we latch on to what other people are doing is that we are confused about how admiration works. Just because you admire something doesn't mean you have to adopt it as your own. It's like when you take a small child on a walk and they want to bring home everything they see. The dandelion! This rock! That stick! Before you know it, you're laden with more things than you can manage to carry home with you. You can admire something without picking it up.

● ● ●

Rebuilding trust in a relationship requires two willing participants. Forgiving a person who isn't sorry won't work. Moving forward without acknowledging what happened won't improve the injuries.

Trusting untrustworthy people will result in repeated patterns.

● ● ●

Feeling "left out" assumes that you were being considered in the first place. Things aren't always about you. Before you get upset, keep in mind the possibility that you are not being rejected intentionally.

• • •

Try this affirmation:

*I appreciate my nervous system for informing
me about what feels unsafe.*

● ● ●

I once had a car that was a money pit. There was always something wrong with it. In the span of weeks, I'd have to replace the starter, alternator, gasket, and windshield-wiper motor. At some point, the car broke down. I gathered up all my stuff, got out of the car, and left it there. I started getting rides from friends. It didn't make any sense for me to continue to spend time and energy getting it repaired. I knew it was time to let it go.

At what point do we, as human beings, realize that pouring our resources into a situation doesn't make sense anymore? Sometimes, it makes sense to call it quits and move on.

● ● ●

I t's kind to let people know sooner rather than later when you can't be present for them. Waiting until the last minute causes hurt feelings and damages the integrity of the relationship.

• • •

What does privilege look like in your life?

Privilege can look like

▸ *Shopping for groceries without being concerned about the cost*

▸ *Having full-time quality childcare*

▸ *Growing up in a stable household*

● ● ●

When someone has a consistent story about being wronged by multiple people, question the storyteller.

Sometimes, people's views of others align with the narrative they want to perpetuate rather than with what actually happened.

● ● ●

L ife is short:

▸ *Dance without focusing on what others think.*

▸ *Take the trip.*

▸ *Say "I love you" first.*

▸ *Forgive yourself.*

▸ *Wear the bright lipstick.*

▸ *Say yes to the last-minute invitation.*

▸ **Live fully.**

● ● ●

I'm the type of person who . . ." This statement may limit your experiences in life.

You can change your perspective.

You may grow to like things that you used to dislike.

You are capable of change, growth, and renewal.

● ● ●

I t's never your job to determine when something is significant enough for someone else to worry about.

Worries often don't make sense. Knowing this doesn't make it easier for people to release their thoughts, however.

Listen, and wonder what the deeper meaning behind a worry might be. Be gentle with yourself and others when you feel worried.

Stop worry-shaming.

● ● ●

Final Words

Short and impactful was my aim for this book of small doses. Take your time to process your insights without acquiring more and more information on a particular topic. Pause and think deeper. Sometimes, too much information can be overwhelming and unnecessary. This book is meant to give you just enough to curate your thoughts and spark discussion. You are becoming more of yourself day by day. Your story is not complete. You are in a continuous state of growth. Take your time. Revisit the words in this book when needed.

About the Author

Nedra Glover Tawwab, MSW, LCSW, is the author of the best-sellers *Drama Free* and *Set Boundaries, Find Peace,* and a licensed therapist and sought-after relationship expert. She has practiced relationship therapy for fifteen years and is the founder and owner of Kaleidoscope Counseling, a group therapy practice. Every day she helps people create healthy relationships by teaching them how to implement boundaries. Her philosophy is that a lack of boundaries and assertiveness underlies most relationship issues, and her gift is helping people create healthy relationships with themselves and others.

Nedra earned her undergraduate and graduate degrees from Wayne State University in Detroit, Michigan. She has additional certifications in working with families and couples and in perinatal mood and anxiety disorders, plus advanced training for counseling adults who've experienced childhood emotional neglect.

Nedra has appeared as an expert on *Red Table Talk, The Breakfast Club, Good Morning America,* and *CBS Mornings,* to name a few. Her work has been highlighted in *The New York Times, The Guardian,* and *Vice,* and she has appeared on numerous podcasts, including *The School of Greatness, We Can Do Hard Things,* and *Ten Percent Happier.* She hosts the podcast *You Need to Hear This,* and shares practices and reflections for mental health on her popular Instagram account. Nedra currently resides in Charlotte, North Carolina, with her family.

ALSO BY
NEDRA GLOVER TAWWAB